THE NEW TEMPLE SHAKESPEARE

Edited by M. R. Ridley, M.A.

CYMBELINE

by William Shakespeare

London: J. M. DENT & SONS LTD.
New York: E. P. DUTTON & CO. INC.

Editor's General Note

The Text.　The editor has kept before him the aim of presenting to the modern reader the nearest possible approximation to what Shakespeare actually wrote. The text is therefore conservative, and is based on the earliest reliable printed text. But to avoid distraction (*a*) the spelling is modernised, and (*b*) a limited number of universally accepted emendations is admitted without comment. Where a Quarto text exists as well as the First Folio the passages which occur only in the Quarto are enclosed in square brackets [ ] and those which occur only in the Folio in brace brackets { }.

Scene Division.　The rapid continuity of the Elizabethan curtainless production is lost by the 'traditional' scene divisions. Where there is an essential difference of place these scene divisions are retained. Where on the other hand the change of place is insignificant the scene division is indicated only by a space on the page. For ease of reference, however, the 'traditional' division is retained at the head of the page and in line numbering.

Notes.　Passages on which there are notes are indicated by a † in the margin.

Punctuation adheres more closely than has been usual to the 'Elizabethan' punctuation of the early texts. It is often therefore more indicative of the way in which the lines were to be delivered than of their syntactical construction.

Glossaries are arranged on a somewhat novel principle, not alphabetically, but in the order in which the words or phrases occur. The editor is much indebted to Mr J. N. Bryson for his collaboration in the preparation of the glossaries.

v

Preface

The Text. The play appeared for the first time in the First Folio. It is heavily, and often rather oddly, punctuated; there is very little mislineation; there is a certain number of obvious errors, and a larger number of passages where one suspects corruption or dislocation without being able to be sure of it. For the obvious errors I have admitted to the text without comment the accepted, and obviously acceptable, emendations; most of the other passages are commented on in the Notes.

Few editors have been content to accept the whole of the vision in V. iv. as Shakespeare's. Dowden condemned with certainty only the hopeless doggerel of ll. 30-92. Sir Edmund Chambers would reject the whole vision. In this there are certain difficulties, since the opening of the scene is Shakespearean enough, down to the end of Posthumus' first speech; and the last part, after the entry of the gaolers, could hardly have been written by anyone else; unless the interval is filled by something it must be unnaturally brief; and if the whole vision disappears there must disappear with it V. v. 425-58, which again is not unlike Shakespeare. But one may notice that if one starts the 'cut' in V. v. at l. 422, Cymbeline's speech to Lucius will run straight on. The whole of the last act seems to me so inferior to the rest of the play (as though Shakespeare, having moved with delight and ease through some of the most moving and loveliest scenes he ever made, was irked by the necessity for tidying the whole business up to a neat conventional ending), that I should be content to excise the doggerel, and leave the rest to Shakespeare in a mood of journeyman's boredom. Some editors have also expressed

vii

doubts about the song in IV. ii. (mainly because l. 239 implies that Fidele's name is to occur). One can only say that if Shakespeare did not write it he must have wished he had. A finesse of disintegration by Staunton provokes Sir Edmund Chambers to a just but unusual explosiveness : " Staunton distinguished himself by finding the last couplet of each stanza inferior to the rest. God knows why! Disintegration is a constant itch with some minds." The song is deservedly famous, but I am not sure that one point of pure craftsmanship has been sufficiently noticed. It is clear, from their prefatory remarks, that the actors concerned were not singers ; and of all the 'songs' in Shakespeare this least needs to be sung, and lends itself most readily to a speaking delivery.

Date of Composition. Simon Forman saw the play, probably in early 1611, and certainly before the end of that year (when he died), but he does not date his seeing of it, as he does for *The Winter's Tale*, and (more doubtfully) for *Macbeth*. There have been all kinds of attempts to assign two different dates to different portions of the play, mainly on the evidence of supposed inconsistencies in the character of Cloten. The inconsistencies are there, but they seem to me a sandy foundation for conjecture. There is also an undoubted connection between the play and Beaumont and Fletcher's *Philaster*, but no clear method of establishing priority. So that in the upshot we are driven back on internal evidence, which points to 1609-10.

Sources. The historical part comes straight from Holinshed, most of it from the accounts of the relations between Britain and Rome, but the fight in the lane from an account of a similar episode in the Scotch wars with the Danes. For the details, which are very interesting, the reader must be referred to Boswell-Stone's *Shakespeare's Holinshed*. For the 'wager' theme the reference is 'European literature *passim*'; but in particular the *Decameron*, the ninth story of the second day. The various channels by which it may have come to Shakespeare are hardly worth tracing here. The wicked-stepmother-cave-cooking-sleeping-draught theme is of course pure fairy tale, Snow-white and the dwarfs. Erudition has wasted its energies in trying to find Shakespeare's 'source.' Fairy tales were told in the sixteenth as well as the nineteenth or any other century.

Duration of Action. Daniel gives twelve days represented on the stage, with the necessary intervals, for various journeys. I do not think that a detailed analysis helps the dramatic appreciation of the play, whose movement is in any case leisurely and episodic.

Criticism. The play, to most readers, falls into two distinct parts; first, four lovely acts, irradiated by the presence of Imogen, the most moving perhaps of all Shakespeare's heroines, who unites with the patience of Desdemona much more than Desdemona's wits, and something of the fire of Beatrice; and then a fifth act which is a mere stupid huddle of battle, vision, and mechanical recognition.

Hazlitt.[1]—Cymbeline is one of the most delightful of Shakespear's historical plays. It may be considered as a dramatic romance, in which the most striking parts of the story are thrown into the form of a dialogue, and the intermediate circumstances

[1] *Characters of Shakespear's Plays.*

are explained by the different speakers, as occasion renders it necessary. The action is less concentrated in consequence; but the interest becomes more aerial and refined from the principle of perspective introduced into the subject by the imaginary changes of scene as well as by the length of time it occupies. The reading of this play is like going a journey with some uncertain object at the end of it, and in which the suspense is kept up and heightened by the long intervals between each action. Though the events are scattered over such an extent of surface, and relate to such a variety of characters, yet the links which bind the different interests of the story together are never entirely broken. The most straggling and seemingly casual incidents are contrived in such a manner as to lead at last to the most complete developement of the catastrophe. The ease and conscious unconcern with which this is effected only makes the skill more wonderful. The business of the plot evidently thickens in the last act: the story moves forward with increasing rapidity at every step; its various ramifications are drawn from the most distant points to the same centre; the principal characters are brought together, and placed in very critical situations; and the fate of almost every person in the drama is made to depend on the solution of a single circumstance —the answer of Iachimo to the question of Imogen respecting the obtaining of the ring from Posthumus.

We have almost as great an affection for Imogen as she had for Posthumus; and she deserves it better. Of all Shakespear's women she is perhaps the most tender and the most artless. Her incredulity in the opening scene with Iachimo, as to her husband's infidelity, is much the same as Desdemona's backwardness to believe Othello's jealousy. Her answer to the most distressing part of the picture is only, " My lord, I fear, has forgot Britain."

Her readiness to pardon Iachimo's false imputations and his designs against herself, is a good lesson to prudes; and may shew that where there is a real attachment to virtue, it has no need to bolster itself up with an outrageous or affected antipathy to vice.

Swinburne.[1]—The play of plays, which is *Cymbeline*, remains alone to receive the last salute of all my love. . . . Here is depth enough with height enough of tragic beauty and passion, terror and love and pity, to approve the presence of the most tragic Master's hand; subtlety enough of sweet and bitter truth to attest the passage of the mightiest and wisest scholar or teacher in the school of the human spirit; beauty with delight enough and glory of life and grace of nature to proclaim the advent of the one omnipotent Maker among all who bear that name. Here above all is the most heavenly triad of human figures that ever even Shakespeare brought together; a diviner three, as it were a living god-garland of the noblest earth-born brothers and love-worthiest heaven-born sister, than the very givers of all grace and happiness to their Grecian worshippers of old time over long before. The passion of Posthumus is noble, and potent the poison of Iachimo; Cymbeline has enough for Shakespeare's present purpose of "the king-becoming graces"; but we think first and last of her who was "truest speaker" and those who "called her brother, when she was but their sister; she them brothers, when they were so indeed." The very crown and flower of all her father's daughters,—I do not speak here of her human father, but her divine—the woman above all Shakespeare's women is Imogen. As in Cleopatra we found the incarnate sex, the woman everlasting, so in Imogen we find half glorified already the immortal godhead of womanhood. I

[1] Reprinted from *A Study of Shakespeare* by permission of the publishers, W. Heinemann Ltd.

would fain have some honey in my words at parting—with Shakespeare never, but for ever with these notes on Shakespeare; and I am therefore something more than fain to close my book upon the name of the woman best beloved in all the world of song and all the tide of time; upon the name of Shakespeare's Imogen.

CYMBELINE

DRAMATIS PERSONÆ

CYMBELINE, *king of Britain.*

CLOTEN, *son to the Queen by a former husband.*

POSTHUMUS LEONATUS, *a gentleman, husband to Imogen.*

BELARIUS, *a banished lord, disguised under the name of Morgan.*

GUIDERIUS, } *sons to Cymbeline, disguised under the names of*
ARVIRAGUS, } *Polydore and Cadwal, supposed sons to Morgan.*

PHILARIO, *friend to Posthumus,* } *Italians.*
IACHIMO, *friend to Philario,* }

CAIUS LUCIUS, *General of the Roman Forces.*

PISANIO, *servant to Posthumus.*

CORNELIUS, *a physician.*

A Roman Captain.

Two Lords of Cymbeline's court.

Two Gentlemen of the same.

Two Gaolers.

QUEEN, wife to Cymbeline.

IMOGEN, *daughter to Cymbeline by a former queen.*

HELEN, *a lady attending on Imogen.*

Lords, Ladies, Roman Senators, Tribunes, a Soothsayer, a Dutchman, a Spaniard, Musicians, Officers, Captains, Soldiers, Messengers, and other Attendants.

Apparitions.

SCENE : *Britain ; Rome.*

CYMBELINE

Act First

SCENE I

Britain.   The garden of Cymbeline's palace

Enter two Gentlemen

1.*G.* You do not meet a man but frowns : our bloods †
    No more obey the heavens than our courtiers
    Still seem as does the king.

2.*G.*   But what's the matter ?

1.*G.* His daughter, and the heir of 's kingdom, whom
    He purpos'd to his wife's sole son—a widow
    That late he married—hath referr'd herself
    Unto a poor but worthy gentleman : she 's wedded,
    Her husband banish'd, she imprison'd : all
    Is outward sorrow, though I think the king
    Be touch'd at very heart.

2.*G.*   None but the king ?   10

1.*G.* He that hath lost her too : so is the queen,
    That most desir'd the match : but not a courtier,
    Although they wear their faces to the bent
    Of the king's looks, hath a heart that is not

1

     Glad at the thing they scowl at.

2.*G.*   And why so ?

1.*G.* He that hath miss'd the princess is a thing
     Too bad for bad report : and he that hath her,
     (I mean, that married her, alack, good man,
     And therefore banish'd) is a creature such
     As, to seek through the regions of the earth   20
     For one his like, there would be something failing
     In him that should compare.   I do not think
     So fair an outward, and such stuff within
     Endows a man but he.

2.*G.*   You speak him far.

1.*G.* I do extend him, sir, within himself,
     Crush him together, rather than unfold
     His measure duly.

2.*G.*   What's his name and birth ?

1.*G.* I cannot delve him to the root : his father
     Was call'd Sicilius, who did join his honour
     Against the Romans with Cassibelan,
     But had his titles by Tenantius, whom   30
     He serv'd with glory and admir'd success ;   †
     So gain'd the sur-addition Leonatus :
     And had (besides this gentleman in question)
     Two other sons, who in the wars o' the time
     Died with their swords in hand ; for which their father,

Then old and fond of issue, took such sorrow
That he quit being ; and his gentle lady,
Big of this gentleman, our theme, deceas'd
As he was born.   The king he takes the babe   40
To his protection, calls him Posthumus Leonatus,
Breeds him, and makes him of his bed-chamber,
Puts to him all the learnings that his time
Could make him the receiver of, which he took,
As we do air, fast as 'twas minister'd,
And in's spring became a harvest : liv'd in court
(Which rare it is to do) most prais'd, most lov'd,
A sample to the youngest ; to the more mature
A glass that feated them ; and to the graver   †
A child that guided dotards ; to his mistress,   50
For whom he now is banish'd, her own price
Proclaims how she esteem'd him ; and his virtue
By her election may be truly read,
What kind of man he is.

2.*G.*   I honour him,
Even out of your report.   But, pray you, tell me,
Is she sole child to the king ?

1.*G.*   His only child.
He had two sons (if this be worth your hearing,
Mark it) the eldest of them at three years old,
I' the swathing clothes the other, from their nursery

Were stolen, and to this hour no guess in knowledge   60
Which way they went.

2.G.   How long is this ago ?

1.G. Some twenty years.

2.G. That a king's children should be so convey'd !
So slackly guarded ! and the search so slow,
That could not trace them !

1.G.   Howsoe'er 'tis strange,
Or that the negligence may well be laugh'd at,
Yet is it true, sir.

2.G.   I do well believe you.

1.G. We must forbear : here comes the gentleman,
The queen, and princess.   *Exeunt*

Enter the Queen, Posthumus and Imogen

Qu. No, be assur'd you shall not find me, daughter,   70
After the slander of most stepmothers,
Evil-ey'd unto you : you're my prisoner, but
Your gaoler shall deliver you the keys
That lock up your restraint.   For you, Posthumus,
So soon as I can win the offended king,
I will be known your advocate : marry, yet
The fire of rage is in him, and 'twere good
You lean'd unto his sentence, with what patience
Your wisdom may inform you.

Post.   Please your highness,

4

I will from hence to-day.

Qu.   You know the peril.   80

I'll fetch a turn about the garden, pitying
The pangs of barr'd affections, though the king
Hath charg'd you should not speak together.   *Exit*

Imo.   O

Dissembling courtesy !   How fine this tyrant
Can tickle where she wounds !   My dearest husband,
I something fear my father's wrath, but nothing
(Always reserv'd my holy duty) what
His rage can do on me : you must be gone,
And I shall here abide the hourly shot
Of angry eyes ; not comforted to live,   90
But that there is this jewel in the world,
That I may see again.

Post.   My queen ! my mistress !

O lady, weep no more, lest I give cause
To be suspected of more tenderness
Than doth become a man !   I will remain
The loyal'st husband that did e'er plight troth :
My residence in Rome at one Philario's,
Who to my father was a friend, to me
Known but by letter : thither write, my queen,
And with mine eyes I'll drink the words you send, 100
Though ink be made of gall.

Re-enter Queen

Qu.   Be brief, I pray you :
If the king come, I shall incur I know not
How much of his displeasure. (*aside*) Yet I'll
    move him
To walk this way : I never do him wrong
But he does buy my injuries, to be friends ;
Pays dear for my offences.   *Exit*

Post.   Should we be taking leave
As long a term as yet we have to live,
The loathness to depart would grow. Adieu !

Imo. Nay, stay a little :
Were you but riding forth to air yourself,   110
Such parting were too petty. Look here, love,
This diamond was my mother's : take it, heart,
But keep it till you woo another wife,
When Imogen is dead.

Post.   How, how ? another ?
You gentle gods, give me but this I have,
And sear up my embracements from a next,   †
With bonds of death ! (*Putting on the ring.*) Remain,
    remain thou here,
While sense can keep it on ! And, sweetest, fairest,
As I my poor self did exchange for you
To your so infinite loss, so in our trifles   120

6

I still win of you : for my sake wear this,
It is a manacle of love, I 'll place it
Upon this fairest prisoner.

> *Putting a bracelet on her arm*

Imo.   O the gods !
When shall we see again ?

> *Enter Cymbeline and Lords*

Post.   Alack, the king !
Cym. Thou basest thing, avoid hence, from my sight !
If after this command thou fraught the court
With thy unworthiness, thou diest : away !
Thou 'rt poison to my blood.

Post.   The gods protect you,
And bless the good remainders of the court !
I am gone.   *Exit*

Imo.   There cannot be a pinch in death   130
More sharp than this is.

Cym.   O disloyal thing,
That shouldst repair my youth, thou heap'st
A year's age on me !

Imo.   I beseech you, sir,
Harm not yourself with your vexation :
I am senseless of your wrath ; a touch more rare
Subdues all pangs, all fears.

Cym.   Past grace ? obedience ?

7

Imo. Past hope, and in despair ; that way, past grace.

Cym. That mightst have had the sole son of my queen !

Imo. O blessed, that I might not !   I chose an eagle,
And did avoid a puttock.   140

Cym. Thou took'st a beggar ; wouldst have made my throne
A seat for baseness.

Imo.   No ; I rather added
A lustre to it.

Cym.   O thou vile one !

Imo.   Sir,
It is your fault that I have lov'd Posthumus :
You bred him as my playfellow, and he is
A man worth any woman ; overbuys me
Almost the sum he pays.

Cym.   What ? art thou mad ?

Imo. Almost, sir : heaven restore me !   Would I were
A neat-herd's daughter, and my Leonatus
Our neighbour-shepherd's son !

Cym.   Thou foolish thing ! 150

Re-enter Queen

They were again together : you have done
Not after our command.   Away with her,
And pen her up.

Qu.   Beseech your patience.   Peace,
Dear lady daughter, peace !   Sweet sovereign,

Leave us to ourselves, and make yourself some
    comfort
Out of your best advice.

Cym.   Nay, let her languish
A drop of blood a day ; and, being ag'd,
Die of this folly !   *Exeunt Cymbeline and Lords*

Qu.   Fie ! you must give way.

               Enter Pisanio

Here is your servant.   How now, sir ?   What news ?

Pis. My lord your son drew on my master.

Qu.   Ha !   160
No harm, I trust, is done ?

Pis.   There might have been
But that my master rather play'd than fought,
And had no help of anger : they were parted
By gentlemen at hand.

Qu.   I am very glad on' t.

Imo. Your son 's my father's friend ; he takes his part
To draw upon an exile !   O brave sir !
I would they were in Afric both together ;
Myself by with a needle, that I might prick
The goer-back.   Why came you from your master ?

Pis. On his command : he would not suffer me   170
To bring him to the haven : left these notes
Of what commands I should be subject to

When't pleas'd you to employ me.

Qu.   This hath been
Your faithful servant : I dare lay mine honour
He will remain so.

Pis.   I humbly thank your highness.

Qu. Pray, walk awhile.

Imo.   About some half-hour hence,
I pray you, speak with me : you shall at least
Go see my lord aboard : for this time leave me.

                                                    Exeunt

SCENE II

The same.   A public place

Enter Cloten and two Lords

1.L. Sir, I would advise you to shift a shirt ; the violence
of action hath made you reek as a sacrifice : where
air comes out, air comes in : there's none abroad so
wholesome as that you vent.

Clo. If my shirt were bloody, then to shift it.   Have I
hurt him ?

2.L. *(aside)* No, faith ; not so much as his patience.

1.L. Hurt him ? his body's a passable carcass, if he be
not hurt : it is a throughfare for steel, if it be not
hurt.   10

2.*L.* (*aside*) His steel was in debt, it went o' the backside the town.

Clo. The villain would not stand me.

2.*L.* (*aside*) No, but he fled forward still, toward your face.

1.*L.* Stand you !   You have land enough of your own ; but he added to your having ; gave you some ground.

2.*L.* (*aside*) As many inches as you have oceans.   Puppies ! †

Clo. I would they had not come between us.

2.*L.* (*aside*) So would I, till you had measur'd how long   20 a fool you were upon the ground.

Clo. And that she should love this fellow, and refuse me !

2.*L.* (*aside*) If it be a sin to make a true election, she is damn'd.

1.*L.* Sir, as I told you always, her beauty and her brain go not together : she 's a good sign, but I have seen small reflection of her wit.

2.*L.* (*aside*) She shines not upon fools, lest the reflection should hurt her.

Clo. Come, I 'll to my chamber.   Would there had been   30 some hurt done !

2.*L.* (*aside*) I wish not so, unless it had been the fall of an ass, which is no great hurt.

Clo. You 'll go with us ?

1.*L.* I 'll attend your lordship.

Clo. Nay, come, let 's go together.
2.L. Well, my lord.   *Exeunt*

SCENE III

A room in Cymbeline's palace

Enter Imogen and Pisanio

Imo. I would thou grew'st unto the shores o' the haven,
And question'dst every sail : if he should write
And I not have it, 'twere a paper lost,
As offer'd mercy is.   What was the last
That he spake to thee ?

Pis.   It was, his queen, his queen !

Imo. Then wav'd his handkerchief ?

Pis.   And kiss'd it, madam.

Imo. Senseless linen, happier therein than I !
And that was all ?

Pis.   No, madam ; for so long
As he could make me with this eye or ear
Distinguish him from others, he did keep   **10**
The deck, with glove, or hat, or handkerchief,
Still waving, as the fits and stirs of 's mind
Could best express how slow his soul sail'd on,
How swift his ship.

Imo.   Thou shouldst have made him

As little as a crow, or less, ere left
To after-eye him.

Pis.   Madam, so I did.

Imo. I would have broke mine eye-strings, crack'd them, but
To look upon him, till the diminution
Of space had pointed him sharp as my needle;
Nay, follow'd him, till he had melted from   20
The smallness of a gnat to air; and then
Have turn'd mine eye, and wept.   But, good Pisanio,
When shall we hear from him?

Pis.   Be assur'd, madam,
With his next vantage.

Imo. I did not take my leave of him, but had
Most pretty things to say: ere I could tell him
How I would think on him at certain hours,
Such thoughts and such; or I could make him swear
The shes of Italy should not betray
Mine interest, and his honour; or have charg'd him,   30
At the sixth hour of morn, at noon, at midnight,
To encounter me with orisons, for then
I am in heaven for him; or ere I could
Give him that parting kiss, which I had set
Betwixt two charming words, comes in my father,
And, like the tyrannous breathing of the north,
Shakes all our buds from growing.

Enter a Lady

Lady. The queen, madam,
Desires your highness' company.

Imo. Those things I bid you do, get them dispatch'd.
I will attend the queen.

Pis. Madam, I shall. *Exeunt* 40

SCENE IV

Rome. Philario's house

*Enter Philario, Iachimo, a Frenchman, a Dutchman,
and a Spaniard*

Iac. Believe it, sir, I have seen him in Britain ; he was
then of a crescent note, expected to prove so worthy
as since he hath been allow'd the name of : but I
could then have look'd on him without the help of
admiration, though the catalogue of his endowments
had been tabled by his side, and I to peruse him by
items.

Phi. You speak of him when he was less furnish'd than
now he is with that which makes him both without
and within. 10

Fre. I have seen him in France : we had very many there
could behold the sun with as firm eyes as he.

Iac. This matter of marrying his king's daughter, wherein

14

he must be weigh'd rather by her value than his own, words him, I doubt not, a great deal from the matter.

Fre. And then his banishment.

Iac. Ay, and the approbation of those that weep this lamentable divorce under her colours are wonderfully to extend him, be it but to fortify her judgement, which else an easy battery might lay flat, for 20 taking a beggar without less quality. But how comes it he is to sojourn with you ? how creeps acquaintance ?

Phi. His father and I were soldiers together, to whom I have been often bound for no less than my life. Here comes the Briton : let him be so entertained amongst you as suits, with gentlemen of your knowing, to a stranger of his quality.

Enter Posthumus

I beseech you all, be better known to this gentleman, whom I commend to you as a noble friend of mine : 30 how worthy he is I will leave to appear hereafter, rather than story him in his own hearing.

Fre. Sir, we have known together in Orleans.

Post. Since when I have been debtor to you for courtesies, which I will be ever to pay, and yet pay still.

Fre. Sir, you o'er-rate my poor kindness ; I was glad I did atone my countryman and you ; it had been

pity you should have been put together with so
mortal a purpose as then each bore, upon importance
of so slight and trivial a nature.   40

*Post.*By your pardon, sir, I was then a young traveller;
rather shunn'd to go even with what I heard, than
in my every action to be guided by others' experi-
ences : but upon my mended judgement (if I offend
not to say it is mended) my quarrel was not altogether
slight.

Fre. Faith, yes, to be put to the arbitrement of swords,
and by such two that would, by all likelihood, have
confounded one the other, or have fallen both.

Iac. Can we with manners ask what was the difference ?   50

Fre. Safely, I think : 'twas a contention in public, which
may without contradiction suffer the report. It
was much like an argument that fell out last night,
where each of us fell in praise of our country mis-
tresses ; this gentleman at that time vouching (and
upon warrant of bloody affirmation) his to be more
fair, virtuous, wise, chaste, constant, qualified, and †
less attemptable than any the rarest of our ladies in
France.

Iac. That lady is not now living ; or this gentleman's   60
opinion, by this, worn out.

*Post.*She holds her virtue still, and I my mind.

Iac. You must not so far prefer her 'fore ours of Italy.

Post. Being so far provok'd as I was in France, I would
abate her nothing, though I profess myself her
adorer, not her friend.

Iac. As fair and as good—a kind of hand-in-hand comparison—had been something too fair and too good
for any lady in Britany.   If she went before others
I have seen, as that diamond of yours outlustres   70
many I have beheld, I could not but believe she
excelled many : but I have not seen the most precious
diamond that is, nor you the lady.

Post. I prais'd her as I rated her : so do I my stone.

Iac. What do you esteem it at ?

Post. More than the world enjoys.

Iac. Either your unparagon'd mistress is dead, or she 's
outpriz'd by a trifle.

Post. You are mistaken : the one may be sold or given,
if there were wealth enough for the purchases, or   80
merit for the gift : the other is not a thing for sale,
and only the gift of the gods.

Iac. Which the gods have given you ?

Post. Which, by their graces, I will keep.

Iac. You may wear her in title yours : but you know
strange fowl light upon neighbouring ponds.
Your ring may be stolen too : so your brace of

unprizable estimations, the one is but frail, and the
other casual; a cunning thief, or a (that way)
accomplished courtier, would hazard the winning 90
both of first and last.

Post. Your Italy contains none so accomplish'd a courtier
to convince the honour of my mistress; if, in the
holding or loss of that, you term her frail. I do
nothing doubt you have store of thieves, notwith-
standing, I fear not my ring.

Phi. Let us leave here, gentlemen.

Post. Sir, with all my heart. This worthy signior, I
thank him, makes no stranger of me; we are
familiar at first.   100

Iac. With five times so much conversation, I should get
ground of your fair mistress; make her go back
even to the yielding, had I admittance and opportunity to friend.

Post. No, no.

Iac. I dare thereupon pawn the moiety of my estate, to
your ring, which in my opinion o'ervalues it something: but I make my wager rather against your
confidence than her reputation: and, to bar your
offence herein too, I durst attempt it against any 110
lady in the world.

Post. You are a great deal abus'd in too bold a persuasion,

and I doubt not you sustain what you 're worthy of
by your attempt.

Iac. What 's that ?

Post. A repulse : though your attempt, as you call it,
deserve more ; a punishment too.

Phi. Gentlemen, enough of this, it came in too suddenly,
let it die as it was born, and I pray you be better
acquainted.   120

Iac. Would I had put my estate and my neighbour's on
the approbation of what I have spoke !

Post. What lady would you choose to assail ?

Iac. Yours, whom in constancy you think stands so safe.
I will lay you ten thousand ducats to your ring, that,
commend me to the court where your lady is, with
no more advantage than the opportunity of a second
conference, and I will bring from thence that honour
of hers, which you imagine so reserv'd.

Post. I will wage against your gold, gold to it : my ring I 130
hold dear as my finger, 'tis part of it.

Iac. You are afraid, and therein the wiser. If you buy
ladies' flesh at a million a dram, you cannot preserve
it from tainting : but I see you have some religion
in you, that you fear.

Post. This is but a custom in your tongue ; you beat a
graver purpose, I hope.

Iac. I am the master of my speeches, and would undergo what 's spoken, I swear.

Post. Will you ? I shall but lend my diamond till your 140 return : let there be covenants drawn between 's : my mistress exceeds in goodness the hugeness of your unworthy thinking : I dare you to this match : here 's my ring.

Phi. I will have it no lay.

Iac. By the gods, it is one. If I bring you no sufficient testimony that I have enjoy'd the dearest bodily part of your mistress, my ten thousand ducats are yours, so is your diamond too, if I come off, and leave her in such honour as you have trust in, she 150 your jewel, this your jewel, and my gold are yours ; provided I have your commendation for my more free entertainment.

Post. I embrace these conditions, let us have articles betwixt us : only, thus far you shall answer : if you make your voyage upon her, and give me directly to understand you have prevail'd, I am no further your enemy ; she is not worth our debate : if she remain unseduc'd, you not making it appear otherwise, for your ill opinion, and the assault you have made to 160 her chastity, you shall answer me with your sword.

Iac. Your hand, a covenant : we will have these things

set down by lawful counsel, and straight away for
Britain, lest the bargain should catch cold and
starve : I will fetch my gold, and have our two
wagers recorded.

*Post.*Agreed.   *Exeunt Posthumus and Iachimo*

Fre. Will this hold, think you ?

Phi. Signior Iachimo will not from it.   Pray let us follow
'em.   *Exeunt* 170

SCENES V AND VI

Britain.   Cymbeline's palace

Enter Queen, Ladies, and Cornelius

Qu. Whiles yet the dew's on ground, gather those
      flowers ;
      Make haste : who has the note of them ?

1.L.   I madam.

Qu. Dispatch.   *Exeunt Ladies*
      Now, master doctor, have you brought those drugs ?

Cor. Pleaseth your highness, ay : here they are, madam :
                              Presenting a small box
       But I beseech your grace, without offence
       (My conscience bids me ask) wherefore you have
       Commanded of me these most poisonous compounds,

21

Which are the movers of a languishing death,
But, though slow, deadly.

Qu.   I wonder, doctor,   10
Thou ask'st me such a question.   Have I not been
Thy pupil long?   Hast thou not learn'd me how
To make perfumes? distil? preserve? yea, so
That our great king himself doth woo me oft
For my confections?   Having thus far proceeded,
(Unless thou think'st me devilish) is 't not meet
That I did amplify my judgement in
Other conclusions?   I will try the forces
Of these thy compounds on such creatures as
We count not worth the hanging, but none human,   20
To try the vigour of them, and apply
Allayments to their act, and by them gather
Their several virtues and effects.

Cor.   Your highness
Shall from this practice but make hard your heart:
Besides, the seeing these effects will be
Both noisome and infectious.

Qu.   O, content thee.
Enter Pisanio
(*aside*) Here comes a flattering rascal; upon him
Will I first work: he 's for his master,
And enemy to my son.   How now, Pisanio!

Doctor, your service for this time is ended, 30
Take your own way.

Cor. (*aside*) I do suspect you, madam,
But you shall do no harm.

Qu. (*to Pisanio*) Hark thee, a word.

Cor. (*aside*) I do not like her. She doth think she has
Strange lingering poisons : I do know her spirit,
And will not trust one of her malice with
A drug of such damn'd nature. Those she has
Will stupefy and dull the sense awhile,
Which first, perchance, she'll prove on cats and dogs,
Then afterward up higher : but there is
No danger in what show of death it makes, 40
More than the locking up the spirits a time,
To be more fresh, reviving. She is fool'd
With a most false effect ; and I the truer,
So to be false with her.

Qu. No further service, doctor,
Until I send for thee.

Cor. I humbly take my leave. *Exit*

Qu. Weeps she still, say'st thou ? Dost thou think in time
She will not quench, and let instructions enter
Where folly now possesses ? Do thou work :
When thou shalt bring me word she loves my son,
I'll tell thee on the instant thou art then 50

As great as is thy master ; greater, for
His fortunes all lie speechless, and his name
Is at last gasp : return he cannot, nor
Continue where he is : to shift his being
Is to exchange one misery with another,
And every day that comes, comes to decay
A day's work in him.   What shalt thou expect,
To be depender on a thing that leans ?
Who cannot be new built, nor has no friends,
So much as but to prop him ?   (*The Queen drops the
    box : Pisanio takes it up.*)   Thou tak'st up   60
Thou know'st not what ; but take it for thy labour :
It is a thing I made, which hath the king
Five times redeem'd from death : I do not know
What is more cordial : nay, I prithee, take it,
It is an earnest of a farther good
That I mean to thee.   Tell thy mistress how
The case stands with her ; do't as from thyself.
Think what a chance thou changest on, but think
Thou hast thy mistress still, to boot, my son,
Who shall take notice of thee : I'll move the king   70
To any shape of thy preferment, such
As thou'lt desire ; and then myself, I chiefly,
That set thee on to this desert, am bound
To load thy merit richly.   Call my women :

Think on my words.   *Exit Pisanio*

                A sly and constant knave,
Not to be shak'd : the agent for his master ;
And the remembrancer of her, to hold
The hand-fast to her lord.   I have given him that
Which, if he take, shall quite unpeople her
Of liegers for her sweet ; and which she after,   80
Except she bend her humour, shall be assur'd
To taste of too.

          Re-enter Pisanio with Ladies

            So, so ; well done, well done :
The violets, cowslips, and the primroses,
Bear to my closet.   Fare thee well, Pisanio ;
Think on my words.   *Exeunt Queen and Ladies*

Pis.   And shall do :
But when to my good lord I prove untrue,
I 'll choke myself : there 's all I 'll do for you.   *Exit*

          Enter Imogen alone

Imo. A father cruel, and a step-dame false,
    A foolish suitor to a wedded lady,
    That hath her husband banish'd ;—O, that husband !

My supreme crown of grief, and those repeated
Vexations of it ! Had I been thief-stol'n,
As my two brothers, happy ! but most miserable
Is the desire that's glorious : blest be those,
How mean soe'er, that have their honest wills,
Which seasons comfort. Who may this be ? Fie !

Enter Pisanio and Iachimo

Pis. Madam, a noble gentleman of Rome,   10
Comes from my lord with letters.

Iac.   Change you, madam ?
The worthy Leonatus is in safety,
And greets your highness dearly.   *Presents a letter*

Imo.   Thanks, good sir.
You're kindly welcome.

Iac. (*aside*) All of her, that is out of door, most rich !
If she be furnish'd with a mind so rare,
She is alone the Arabian bird ; and I
Have lost the wager. Boldness be my friend !
Arm me, audacity, from head to foot !
Or, like the Parthian, I shall flying fight,   20
Rather, directly fly.

Imo. (*reads*) 'He is one of the noblest note, to whose
kindnesses I am most infinitely tied. Reflect upon
him accordingly, as you value your trust—

                      LEONATUS.'

So far I read aloud :
But even the very middle of my heart
Is warm'd by the rest, and takes it thankfully.
You are as welcome, worthy sir, as I
Have words to bid you, and shall find it so   30
In all that I can do.

Iac.   Thanks, fairest lady.
What, are men mad ?   Hath nature given them eyes
To see this vaulted arch, and the rich crop
Of sea and land, which can distinguish 'twixt
The fiery orbs above and the twinn'd stones
Upon the number'd beach, and can we not   †
Partition make with spectacles so precious
'Twixt fair and foul ?

Imo.   What makes your admiration ?
Iac. It cannot be i' the eye ; for apes and monkeys,
'Twixt two such shes, would chatter this way and   40
Contemn with mows the other : nor i' the judge-
          ment ;
For idiots, in this case of favour, would
Be wisely definite : nor i' the appetite ;
Sluttery, to such neat excellence oppos'd,
Should make desire vomit emptiness,
Not so allur'd to feed.

Imo. What is the matter, trow ?

Iac.   The cloyed will,
That satiate yet unsatisfied desire, that tub
Both fill'd and running, ravening first the lamb.
Longs after for the garbage.

Imo.   What, dear sir,   50
Thus raps you ?   Are you well ?

Iac.   Thanks, madam, well.
(*to Pisanio*) Beseech you, sir,
Desire my man's abode where I did leave him :
He's strange and peevish.

Pis.   I was going, sir,
To give him welcome.   *Exit*

Imo. Continues well my lord ?   His health, beseech you ?

Iac. Well, madam.

Imo. Is he dispos'd to mirth ?   I hope he is.

Iac. Exceeding pleasant ; none a stranger there
So merry and so gamesome : he is call'd   60
The Briton reveller.

Imo.   When he was here
He did incline to sadness, and oft-times
Not knowing why.

Iac.   I never saw him sad.
There is a Frenchman his companion, one
An eminent monsieur, that, it seems, much loves
A Gallian girl at home : he furnaces

The thick sighs from him ; whiles the jolly Briton,
Your lord, I mean, laughs from 's free lungs, cries ' O,
Can my sides hold, to think that man, who knows
By history, report, or his own proof,   70
What woman is, yea, what she cannot choose
But must be, will his free hours languish for
Assured bondage ? '

Imo.   Will my lord say so ?

Iac. Ay, madam ; with his eyes in flood with laughter
It is a recreation to be by
And hear him mock the Frenchman.   But, heavens
     know,
Some men are much to blame.

Imo.   Not he, I hope.

Iac. Not he : but yet heaven's bounty towards him might
Be us'd more thankfully.   In himself 'tis much ;
In you, which I account his beyond all talents,   80
Whilst I am bound to wonder, I am bound
To pity too.

Imo.   What do you pity, sir ?

Iac. Two creatures heartily.

Imo.   Am I one, sir ?
You look on me : what wreck discern you in me
Deserves your pity ?

Iac.   Lamentable !   What,

29

  To hide me from the radiant sun, and solace
  I' the dungeon by a snuff?

Imo.   I pray you, sir,
  Deliver with more openness your answers
  To my demands. Why do you pity me?

Iac. That others do,   90
  (I was about to say) enjoy your——But
  It is an office of the gods to venge it,
  Not mine to speak on 't.

Imo.   You do seem to know
  Something of me, or what concerns me : pray you,
  Since doubting things go ill, often hurts more
  Than to be sure they do ; for certainties
  Either are past remedies, or, timely knowing,
  The remedy then born, discover to me
  What both you spur and stop.

Iac.   Had I this cheek
  To bathe my lips upon ; this hand, whose touch, 100
  Whose every touch, would force the feeler's soul
  To the oath of loyalty ; this object, which
  Takes prisoner the wild motion of mine eye,
  Fixing it only here ; should I, damn'd then, †
  Slaver with lips as common as the stairs
  That mount the Capitol ; join gripes with hands
  Made hard with hourly falsehood (falsehood, as

        With labour ;) then by-peeping in an eye
        Base and unlustrous as the smoky light   †
        That's fed with stinking tallow ; it were fit   110
        That all the plagues of hell should at one time
        Encounter such revolt.

Imo.   My lord, I fear,
        Has forgot Britain.

Iac.   And himself.   Not I
        Inclin'd to this intelligence pronounce
        The beggary of his change ; but 'tis your graces
        That from my mutest conscience to my tongue
        Charms this report out.

Imo.   Let me hear no more.

Iac. O dearest soul, your cause doth strike my heart
        With pity, that doth make me sick !   A lady
        So fair, and fasten'd to an empery,   120
        Would make the great'st king double, to be partner'd   †
        With tomboys hir'd with that self exhibition
        Which your own coffers yield ! with diseas'd ventures
        That play with all infirmities for gold
        Which rottenness can lead nature ! such boil'd stuff
        As well might poison poison !   Be reveng'd,
        Or she that bore you was no queen, and you
        Recoil from your great stock.

Imo.   Reveng'd !

                            31

How should I be reveng'd ? If this be true,
(As I have such a heart that both mine ears   130
Must not in haste abuse) if it be true,
How should I be reveng'd ?

Iac.   Should he make me
Live like Diana's priest, betwixt cold sheets,
Whiles he is vaulting variable ramps,
In your despite, upon your purse ? Revenge it.
I dedicate myself to your sweet pleasure,
More noble than that runagate to your bed,
And will continue fast to your affection,
Still close as sure.

Imo.   What ho, Pisanio !

Iac. Let me my service tender on your lips.   140

Imo. Away ! I do condemn mine ears, that have
So long attended thee. If thou wert honourable,
Thou wouldst have told this tale for virtue, not
For such an end thou seek'st, as base as strange.
Thou wrong'st a gentleman who is as far
From thy report as thou from honour ; and
Solicits here a lady that disdains
Thee and the devil alike. What ho, Pisanio !
The king my father shall be made acquainted
Of thy assault : if he shall think it fit   150
A saucy stranger in his court to mart

As in a Romish stew, and to expound
His beastly mind to us, he hath a court
He little cares for, and a daughter who
He not respects at all.   What ho, Pisanio !

Iac. O happy Leonatus !   I may say,
The credit that thy lady hath of thee
Deserves thy trust, and thy most perfect goodness
Her assur'd credit.   Blessed live you long !
A lady to the worthiest sir that ever   160
Country call'd his ! and you his mistress, only
For the most worthiest fit !   Give me your pardon ;
I have spoke this to know if your affiance
Were deeply rooted, and shall make your lord
That which he is new o'er : and he is one
The truest manner'd, such a holy witch,
That he enchants societies into him ;
Half all men's hearts are his.

Imo.   You make amends.

Iac. He sits 'mongst men like a descended god :
He hath a kind of honour sets him off,   170
More than a mortal seeming.   Be not angry,
Most mighty princess, that I have adventur'd
To try your taking of a false report, which hath
Honour'd with confirmation your great judgement
In the election of a sir so rare,

Which you know cannot err.   The love I bear him
Made me to fan you thus, but the gods made you,
Unlike all others, chaffless.   Pray, your pardon.

Imo. All 's well, sir : take my power i' the court for yours.

Iac. My humble thanks.   I had almost forgot   180
To entreat your grace but in a small request,
And yet of moment too, for it concerns
Your lord ; myself, and other noble friends,
Are partners in the business.

Imo.   Pray, what is 't ?

Iac. Some dozen Romans of us, and your lord
(The best feather of our wing) have mingled sums
To buy a present for the emperor ;
Which I, the factor for the rest, have done
In France : 'tis plate of rare device, and jewels
Of rich and exquisite form, their values great,   190
And I am something curious, being strange,
To have them in safe stowage : may it please you
To take them in protection ?

Imo.   Willingly ;
And pawn mine honour for their safety, since
My lord hath interest in them, I will keep them
In my bedchamber.

Iac.   They are in a trunk.
Attended by my men : I will make bold

To send them to you, only for this night ;
I must aboard to-morrow.

Imo.   O, no, no.

Iac. Yes, I beseech ; or I shall short my word   200
By lengthening my return.   From Gallia
I cross'd the seas on purpose, and on promise
To see your grace.

Imo.   I thank you for your pains :
But not away to-morrow !

Iac.   O, I must, madam :
Therefore I shall beseech you, if you please
To greet your lord with writing, do 't to-night :
I have outstood my time, which is material
To the tender of our present.

Imo.   I will write.
Send your trunk to me, it shall safe be kept,
And truly yielded you.   You 're very welcome.   210

Exeunt

Act Second

SCENE I

Britain. Before Cymbeline's palace

Enter Cloten and two Lords

Clo. Was there ever man had such luck! when I kiss'd the jack, upon an up-cast to be hit away! I had a hundred pound on 't: and then a whoreson jackanapes must take me up for swearing; as if I borrowed mine oaths of him, and might not spend them at my pleasure.

1.L. What got he by that? You have broke his pate with your bowl.

2.L. (*aside*) If his wit has been like him that broke it, it would have run all out.

Clo. When a gentleman is dispos'd to swear, it is not for any standers-by to curtail his oaths, ha?

2.L. No, my lord; (*aside*) nor crop the ears of them.

Clo. Whoreson dog! I give him satisfaction? Would he had been one of my rank!

2.L. (*aside*) To have smelt like a fool.

Clo. I am not vex'd more at any thing in the earth: a pox on 't! I had rather not be so noble as I am;

10

they dare not fight with me, because of the queen
my mother : every Jack-slave hath his bellyful of   20
fighting, and I must go up and down like a cock
that nobody can match.

2.L. (*aside*) You are cock and capon too, and you crow,
cock, with your comb on.

Clo. Sayest thou ?

2.L. It is not fit your lordship should undertake every
companion that you give offence to.

Clo. No, I know that : but it is fit I should commit
offence to my inferiors.

2.L. Ay, it is fit for your lordship only.   30

Clo. Why, so I say.

1.L. Did you hear of a stranger that's come to court
to-night ?

Clo. A stranger, and I not know on 't ?

2.L. (*aside*) He's a strange fellow himself, and knows
it not.

1.L. There's an Italian come, and 'tis thought, one of
Leonatus' friends.

Clo. Leonatus ? a banish'd rascal ; and he's another,
whatsoever he be.   Who told you of this stranger ?   40

1.L. One of your lordship's pages.

Clo. Is it fit I went to look upon him ? is there no deroga-
tion in 't ?

2.*L.* You cannot derogate, my lord.

Clo. Not easily, I think.

2.*L.* (*aside*) You are a fool granted; therefore your issues, being foolish, do not derogate.

Clo. Come, I'll go see this Italian: what I have lost to-day at bowls I'll win to-night of him. Come, go.

2.*L.* I'll attend your lordship.   50

Exeunt Cloten and First Lord

That such a crafty devil as is his mother
Should yield the world this ass? a woman that
Bears all down with her brain, and this her son
Cannot take two from twenty, for his heart,
And leave eighteen.   Alas, poor princess,
Thou divine Imogen, what thou endur'st,
Betwixt a father by thy step-dame govern'd,
A mother hourly coining plots, a wooer
More hateful than the foul expulsion is
Of thy dear husband, than that horrid act   60
Of the divorce he'ld make !   The heavens hold firm
The walls of thy dear honour ; keep unshak'd
That temple, thy fair mind ; that thou mayst stand,
To enjoy thy banish'd lord, and this great land !

Exit

38

SCENE II

Imogen's bedchamber in Cymbeline's palace;
a trunk in one corner of it

Imogen in bed, reading; a Lady attending

Imo. Who's there? my woman Helen?

Lady.   Please you, madam.

Imo. What hour is it?

Lady.   Almost midnight, madam.

Imo. I have read three hours then: mine eyes are weak:
Fold down the leaf where I have left: to bed:
Take not away the taper, leave it burning;
And if thou canst awake by four o' the clock,
I prithee, call me.   Sleep hath seiz'd me wholly.

                                         Exit Lady

To your protection I commend me, gods!
From fairies, and the tempters of the night,
Guard me, beseech ye!   10

                Sleeps.   Iachimo comes from the trunk

Iac. The crickets sing, and man's o'er-labour'd sense
Repairs itself by rest.   Our Tarquin thus
Did softly press the rushes, ere he waken'd
The chastity he wounded.   Cytherea,
How bravely thou becomest thy bed! fresh lily,

39

And whiter than the sheets !   That I might touch,
But kiss, one kiss !   Rubies unparagon'd,
How dearly they do 't !   'Tis her breathing that   †
Perfumes the chamber thus : the flame o' the taper
Bows toward her, and would under-peep her lids   20
To see the unclosed lights, now canopied
Under those windows, white and azure-lac'd
With blue of heaven's own tinct.   But my design ;
To note the chamber, I will write all down :
Such and such pictures ; there the window ; such
The adornment of her bed ; the arras, figures,
Why, such and such ; and the contents o' the story.
Ah, but some natural notes about her body
Above ten thousand meaner moveables
Would testify, to enrich mine inventory.   30
O sleep, thou ape of death, lie dull upon her,
And be her sense but as a monument,
Thus in a chapel lying !   Come off, come off :

>   *Taking off her bracelet*

As slippery as the Gordian knot was hard !
'Tis mine, and this will witness outwardly,
As strongly as the conscience does within,
To the madding of her lord.   On her left breast
A mole cinque-spotted, like the crimson drops
I' the bottom of a cowslip : here 's a voucher,

40

Stronger than ever law could make ; this secret   40
Will force him think I have pick'd the lock, and ta'en
The treasure of her honour.   No more.   To what
    end ?
Why should I write this down, that 's riveted,
Screw'd to my memory?   She hath been reading late
The tale of Tereus ; here the leaf 's turned down   1
Where Philomel gave up.   I have enough :
To the trunk again, and shut the spring of it.
Swift, swift, you dragons of the night, that dawning
May bare the raven's eye !   I lodge in fear ;
Though this a heavenly angel, hell is here.   50

                                Clock strikes

One, two, three : time, time !
                    Goes into the trunk.   The scene closes

SCENE III

An ante-chamber adjoining Imogen's apartments

Enter Cloten and Lords

1.L. Your lordship is the most patient man in loss, the
    most coldest that ever turn'd up ace.

Clo. It would make any man cold to lose.

1.L. But not every man patient after the noble temper of

your lordship.   You are most hot and furious when
you win.

Clo. Winning will put any man into courage.   If I could
get this foolish Imogen, I should have gold enough.
It 's almost morning, is 't not ?

1.*L.* Day, my lord.   10

Clo. I would this music would come : I am advised to
give her music o' mornings, they say it will penetrate.

Enter Musicians

Come on ; tune : if you can penetrate her with your
fingering, so ; we 'll try with tongue too : if none
will do, let her remain ; but I 'll never give o'er.
First, a very excellent good conceited thing ; after a
wonderful sweet air, with admirable rich words to
it : and then let her consider.

SONG

Hark, hark ! the lark at heaven's gate sings,
   And Phœbus 'gins arise,
His steeds to water at those springs   20
   On chalic'd flowers that lies ;
And winking Mary-buds begin
   To ope their golden eyes ;
With every thing that pretty is,   †
   My lady sweet, arise :
      Arise, arise !

Clo. So, get you gone.   If this penetrate, I will consider
    your music the better : if it do not, it is a vice in her
    ears, which horse-hairs, and calves'-guts, nor the   30
    voice of unpav'd eunuch to boot, can never amend.
                                       Exeunt Musicians

2.L. Here comes the king.

Clo. I am glad I was up so late, for that's the reason I
    was up so early : he cannot choose but take this
    service I have done fatherly.
              Enter Cymbeline and Queen
    Good morrow to your majesty, and to my gracious
    mother.

Cym. Attend you here the door of our stern daughter ?
    Will she not forth ?

Clo. I have assail'd her with music, but she vouchsafes   40
    no notice.

Cym. The exile of her minion is too new,
    She hath not yet forgot him : some more time
    Must wear the print of his remembrance out,
    And then she's yours.

Qu.   You are most bound to the king,
    Who lets go by no vantages that may
    Prefer you to his daughter.   Frame yourself
    To orderly soliciting, and be friended   †
    With aptness of the season : make denials

Increase your services ; so seem as if   50
You were inspir'd to do those duties which
You tender to her ; that you in all obey her,
Save when command to your dismission tends,
And therein you are senseless.

Clo.   Senseless ? not so.

        Enter a Messenger

Mes. So like you, sir, ambassadors from Rome ;
The one is Caius Lucius.

Cym.   A worthy fellow,
Albeit he comes on angry purpose now ;
But that's no fault of his : we must receive him
According to the honour of his sender,
And towards himself, his goodness forespent on us,   60
We must extend our notice. Our dear son,
When you have given good morning to your mistress,
Attend the queen and us ; we shall have need
To employ you towards this Roman. Come, our
    queen.   *Exeunt all but Cloten*

Clo. If she be up, I'll speak with her ; if not,
Let her lie still, and dream. By your leave, ho !
                    Knocks

I know her women are about her : what
If I do line one of their hands ? 'Tis gold
Which buys admittance ; oft it doth ; yea, and makes

44

Diana's rangers false themselves, yield up   70
Their deer to the stand o' the stealer ; and 'tis gold
Which makes the true man kill'd, and saves the thief ;
Nay, sometime hangs both thief and true man : what
Can it not do, and undo ?   I will make
One of her women lawyer to me, for
I yet not understand the case myself.
By your leave.   *Knocks*

Enter a Lady

Lady. Who 's there that knocks ?

Clo.   A gentleman.

Lady.   No more ?

Clo. Yes, and a gentlewoman's son.

Lady.   That 's more
Than some whose tailors are as dear as yours   80
Can justly boast of.   What 's your lordship's pleasure ?

Clo. Your lady's person ; is she ready ?

Lady.   Ay,
To keep her chamber.

Clo.   There is gold for you ;
Sell me your good report.

Lady. How, my good name ? or to report of you
What I shall think is good ?   The princess !

Exit Lady

45

Enter Imogen

Clo. Good morrow, fairest : sister, your sweet hand.

Imo. Good morrow, sir ; you lay out too much pains
    For purchasing but trouble : the thanks I give
    Is telling you that I am poor of thanks,   90
    And scarce can spare them.

Clo.   Still I swear I love you.

Imo. If you but said so, 'twere as deep with me :
    If you swear still, your recompense is still
    That I regard it not.

Clo.   This is no answer.

Imo. But that you shall not say I yield being silent,
    I would not speak. I pray you, spare me : faith,
    I shall unfold equal discourtesy
    To your best kindness : one of your great knowing
    Should learn, being taught, forbearance.

Clo. To leave you in your madness, 'twere my sin :   100
    I will not.

Imo. Fools are not mad folks.

Clo.   Do you call me fool ?

Imo. As I am mad, I do :
    If you'll be patient, I'll no more be mad ;
    That cures us both. I am much sorry, sir,
    You put me to forget a lady's manners.
    By being so verbal : and learn now, for all,

That I, which know my heart, do here pronounce,
By the very truth of it, I care not for you,
And am so near the lack of charity,   110
To accuse myself, I hate you ; which I had rather
You felt than make 't my boast.

Clo.   You sin against
Obedience, which you owe your father ; for
The contract you pretend with that base wretch,
One bred of alms, and foster'd with cold dishes,
With scraps o' the court, it is no contract, none :
And though it be allow'd in meaner parties
(Yet who than he more mean ?) to knit their souls
(On whom there is no more dependency
But brats and beggary) in self-figur'd knot,   120
Yet you are curb'd from that enlargement by
The consequence o' the crown, and must not soil
The precious note of it with a base slave,
A hilding for a livery, a squire's cloth,
A pantler, not so eminent.

Imo.   Profane fellow !
Wert thou the son of Jupiter, and no more
But what thou art besides, thou wert too base
To be his groom : thou wert dignified enough,
Even to the point of envy, if 'twere made
Comparative for your virtues to be styl'd   130

47

        The under-hangman of his kingdom : and hated
        For being preferr'd so well.

Clo.   The south-fog rot him !

Imo. He never can meet more mischance than come
        To be but nam'd of thee. His meanest garment,
        That ever hath but clipp'd his body, is dearer
        In my respect than all the hairs above thee,
        Were they all made such men. How now, Pisanio ?

                   Enter Pisanio

Clo. ' His garment ? ' Now, the devil—

Imo. To Dorothy my woman hie thee presently,—

Clo. ' His garment ! '

Imo.   I am sprited with a fool,   140
        Frighted, and anger'd worse : go bid my woman
        Search for a jewel that too casually
        Hath left mine arm : it was thy master's : 'shrew me,
        If I would lose it for a revenue
        Of any king's in Europe ! I do think
        I saw 't this morning : confident I am
        Last night 'twas on mine arm ; I kiss'd it :
        I hope it be not gone, to tell my lord
        That I kiss aught but he.

Pis.   'Twill not be lost.

Imo. I hope so : go and search.   *Exit Pisanio*

Clo.   You have abus'd me :   150

'His meanest garment?'

Imo.   Ay, I said so, sir:
If you will make't an action, call witness to't.

Clo. I will inform your father.

Imo.   Your mother too:
She's my good lady, and will conceive, I hope,
But the worst of me. So I leave you sir,
To the worst of discontent.   *Exit*

Clo.   I'll be reveng'd:
'His meanest garment?' Well.   *Exit*

SCENES IV AND V

Rome. Philario's house

Enter Posthumus and Philario

*Post.*Fear it not, sir: I would I were so sure
To win the king as I am bold her honour
Will remain hers.

Phi.   What means do you make to him?

*Post.*Not any; but abide the change of time,
Quake in the present winter's state, and wish
That warmer days would come: in these fear'd hopes,
I barely gratify your love; they failing,
I must die much your debtor.

Phi. Your very goodness, and your company,
O'erpays all I can do. By this, your king   10
Hath heard of great Augustus : Caius Lucius
Will do's commission throughly : and I think
He'll grant the tribute, send the arrearages,
Or look upon our Romans, whose remembrance
Is yet fresh in their grief.

Post.   I do believe
(Statist though I am none, nor like to be)
That this will prove a war ; and you shall hear
The legions now in Gallia sooner landed
In our not-fearing Britain than have tidings
Of any penny tribute paid. Our countrymen   20
Are men more order'd than when Julius Cæsar
Smil'd at their lack of skill, but found their courage
Worthy his frowning at : their discipline,
Now mingled with their courage, will make known †
To their approvers they are people such
That mend upon the world.

Enter Iachimo

Phi.   See, Iachimo !
Post. The swiftest harts have posted you by land,
And winds of all the corners kiss'd your sails,
To make your vessel nimble.

Phi.   Welcome, sir.

Post. I hope the briefness of your answer made   30
    The speediness of your return.

Iac.   Your lady
    Is one of the fairest that I have look'd upon.

Post. And therewithal the best, or let her beauty
    Look through a casement to allure false hearts,
    And be false with them.

Iac.   Here are letters for you.

Post. Their tenour good, I trust.

Iac.   'Tis very like.

Phi. Was Caius Lucius in the Britain court
    When you were there ?

Iac.   He was expected then,
    But not approach'd.

Post.   All is well yet.
    Sparkles this stone as it was wont ? or is 't not   40
    Too dull for your good wearing ?

Iac.   If I had lost it,
    I should have lost the worth of it in gold.
    I'll make a journey twice as far, to enjoy
    A second night of such sweet shortness which
    Was mine in Britain ; for the ring is won.

Post. The stone's too hard to come by.

Iac.   Not a whit,
    Your lady being so easy.

Post.   Make not, sir,
　　Your loss your sport : I hope you know that we
　　Must not continue friends.

Iac.   Good sir, we must,
　　If you keep covenant.　Had I not brought   50
　　The knowledge of your mistress home, I grant
　　We were to question farther : but I now
　　Profess myself the winner of her honour,
　　Together with your ring ; and not the wronger
　　Of her or you, having proceeded but
　　By both your wills.

Post.   If you can make't apparent
　　That you have tasted her in bed, my hand
　　And ring is yours : if not, the foul opinion
　　You had of her pure honour gains or loses
　　Your sword or mine, or masterless leaves both   60
　　To who shall find them.

Iac.   Sir, my circumstances,
　　Being so near the truth as I will make them,
　　Must first induce you to believe ; whose strength
　　I will confirm with oath, which, I doubt not,
　　You 'll give me leave to spare, when you shall find
　　You need it not.

Post.   Proceed.

Iac.   First, her bedchamber,

(Where, I confess, I slept not, but profess
Had that was well worth watching) it was hang'd
With tapestry of silk and silver, the story
Proud Cleopatra, when she met her Roman,   70
And Cydnus swell'd above the banks, or for
The press of boats, or pride : a piece of work
So bravely done, so rich, that it did strive
In workmanship and value, which I wonder'd
Could be so rarely and exactly wrought,
Since the true life on 't was—

Post.   This is true ;
And this you might have heard of here, by me,
Or by some other.

Iac.   More particulars
Must justify my knowledge.

Post.   So they must,
Or do your honour injury.

Iac.   The chimney   80
Is south the chamber, and the chimney-piece,
Chaste Dian bathing ; never saw I figures
So likely to report themselves : the cutter   †
Was as another nature, dumb ; outwent her,
Motion and breath left out.

Post.   This is a thing
Which you might from relation likewise reap,

53

Being, as it is, much spoke of.

Iac.   The roof o' the chamber
With golden cherubins is fretted : her andirons
(I had forgot them) were two winking Cupids
Of silver, each on one foot standing, nicely   90
Depending on their brands.

Post.   This is her honour !
Let it be granted you have seen all this (and praise
Be given to your remembrance) the description
Of what is in her chamber nothing saves
The wager you have laid.

Iac.   Then, if you can,

                              Showing the bracelet

Be pale : I beg but leave to air this jewel ; see !
And now 'tis up again : it must be married
To that your diamond ; I 'll keep them.

Post.   Jove !
Once more let me behold it : is it that
Which I left with her ?

Iac.   Sir (I thank her) that :   100
She stripp'd it from her arm ; I see her yet ;
Her pretty action did outsell her gift,
And yet enrich'd it too : she gave it me,
And said, she priz'd it once.

Post.   May be she pluck'd it off

54

To send it me.

Iac.   She writes so to you, doth she ?

*Post.*O, no, no, no ! 'tis true.   Here, take this too,

                                 Gives the ring

It is a basilisk unto mine eye,

Kills me to look on 't.   Let there be no honour

Where there is beauty ; truth, where semblance ; love,

Where there 's another man : the vows of women   110

Of no more bondage be to where they are made

Than they are to their virtues, which is nothing.

O, above measure false !

Phi.   Have patience, sir,

And take your ring again ; 'tis not yet won :

It may be probable she lost it ; or

Who knows if one of her women, being corrupted,

Hath stol'n it from her ?

Post.   Very true,

And so, I hope, he came by 't.   Back my ring,

Render to me some corporal sign about her

More evident than this ; for this was stol'n.   120

Iac. By Jupiter, I had it from her arm.

*Post.*Hark you, he swears ; by Jupiter he swears.

    'Tis true, nay, keep the ring ; 'tis true : I am sure

She would not lose it : her attendants are

All sworn and honourable : they induc'd to steal it ?

And by a stranger ?   No, he hath enjoy'd her :
The cognizance of her incontinency
Is this : she hath bought the name of whore thus dearly.
There, take thy hire, and all the fiends of hell
Divide themselves between you !

Phi.   Sir, be patient :   130
This is not strong enough to be believ'd
Of one persuaded well of—

Post.   Never talk on 't ;
She hath been colted by him.

Iac.   If you seek
For further satisfying, under her breast
(Worthy the pressing) lies a mole, right proud
Of that most delicate lodging : by my life,
I kiss'd it, and it gave me present hunger
To feed again, though full.   You do remember
This stain upon her ?

Post.   Ay, and it doth confirm
Another stain, as big as hell can hold,   140
Were there no more but it.

Iac.   Will you hear more ?

Post. Spare your arithmetic, never count the turns ;
Once, and a million !

Iac.   I 'll be sworn—

Post.   No swearing.

If you will swear you have not done 't, you lie,
And I will kill thee, if thou dost deny
Thou 'st made me cuckold.

Iac.   I 'll deny nothing.

*Post.*O, that I had her here, to tear her limb-meal !
I will go there and do 't, i' the court, before
Her father.   I 'll do something——   *Exit*

Phi.   Quite besides
The government of patience !   You have won: 150
Let 's follow him, and pervert the present wrath
He hath against himself.

Iac.   With all my heart.   *Exeunt*

Enter Posthumus

*Post.*Is there no way for men to be, but women
Must be half-workers ?   We are all bastards,
And that most venerable man which I
Did call my father, was I know not where
When I was stamp'd ; some coiner with his tools
Made me a counterfeit : yet my mother seem'd
The Dian of that time : so doth my wife

The nonpareil of this.   O, vengeance, vengeance!
Me of my lawful pleasure she restrain'd,
And pray'd me oft forbearance; did it with   10
A pudency so rosy, the sweet view on 't
Might well have warm'd old Saturn; that I thought
      her
As chaste as unsunn'd snow.   O, all the devils!
This yellow Iachimo, in an hour, was 't not?
Or less; at first? perchance he spoke not, but
Like a full-acorn'd boar, a German one,   †
Cried 'O!', and mounted; found no opposition
But what he look'd for should oppose, and she
Should from encounter guard.   Could I find out
The woman's part in me!   For there 's no motion   20
That tends to vice in man but I affirm
It is the woman's part: be it lying, note it,
The woman's; flattering, hers; deceiving, hers;
Lust, and rank thoughts, hers, hers; revenges, hers;
Ambitions, covetings, change of prides, disdain,
Nice longing, slanders, mutability,
All faults that may be nam'd, nay, that hell knows,   †
Why, hers, in part or all; but rather all,
For even to vice
They are not constant, but are changing still   30
One vice, but of a minute old, for one

Not half so old as that.   I'll write against them,
Detest them, curse them : yet 'tis greater skill
In a true hate, to pray they have their will :
The very devils cannot plague them better.   *Exit*

Act Third

SCENE I

Britain.   A hall in Cymbeline's palace

*Enter in state, Cymbeline, Queen, Cloten, and Lords at
one door, and at another, Caius Lucius and Attendants*

Cym. Now say, what would Augustus Cæsar with us ?
Luc. When Julius Cæsar (whose remembrance yet
 Lives in men's eyes, and will to ears and tongues
 Be theme and hearing ever) was in this Britain,
 And conquer'd it, Cassibelan, thine uncle,
 (Famous in Cæsar's praises, no whit less
 Than in his feats deserving it) for him,
 And his succession, granted Rome a tribute,
 Yearly three thousand pounds ; which by thee lately
 Is left untender'd.

Qu.   And, to kill the marvel, 10

Shall be so ever.

Clo.   There be many Cæsars,
Ere such another Julius.   Britain is
A world by itself, and we will nothing pay
For wearing our own noses.

Qu.   That opportunity,
Which then they had to take from's, to resume
We have again.   Remember, sir, my liege,
The kings your ancestors, together with
The natural bravery of your isle, which stands
As Neptune's park, ribbed and paled in   †
With rocks unscaleable, and roaring waters,   20
With sands that will not bear your enemies' boats,
But suck them up to the topmast.   A kind of conquest
Cæsar made here, but made not here his brag
Of 'Came, and saw, and overcame:' with shame
(The first that ever touch'd him) he was carried
From off our coast, twice beaten; and his shipping
(Poor ignorant baubles!) on our terrible seas,
Like egg-shells mov'd upon their surges, crack'd
As easily 'gainst our rocks: for joy whereof
The famed Cassibelan, who was once at point   30
(O giglet fortune!) to master Cæsar's sword,
Made Lud's town with rejoicing fires bright
And Britons strut with courage.

Clo. Come, there's no more tribute to be paid: our
kingdom is stronger than it was at that time; and,
as I said, there is no moe such Cæsars: other of
them may have crook'd noses, but to owe such
straight arms, none.

Cym. Son, let your mother end.

Clo. We have yet many among us can gripe as hard as 40
Cassibelan: I do not say I am one; but I have a
hand. Why tribute? why should we pay tribute?
If Cæsar can hide the sun from us with a blanket, or
put the moon in his pocket, we will pay him tribute
for light; else, sir, no more tribute, pray you now.

Cym. You must know,
Till the injurious Romans did extort
This tribute from us, we were free: Cæsar's ambition,
Which swell'd so much that it did almost stretch
The sides o' the world, against all colour here 50
Did put the yoke upon's; which to shake off
Becomes a warlike people, whom we reckon
Ourselves to be.

Clo. and Lords. We do.

Cym.   Say then to Cæsar,
Our ancestor was that Mulmutius which
Ordain'd our laws, whose use the sword of Cæsar
Hath too much mangled; whose repair, and franchise,

Shall, by the power we hold, be our good deed,
Though Rome be therefore angry. Mulmutius
    made our laws,
Who was the first of Britain which did put   60
His brows within a golden crown, and call'd
Himself a king.

Luc.   I am sorry, Cymbeline,
That I am to pronounce Augustus Cæsar
(Cæsar, that hath moe kings his servants than
Thyself domestic officers) thine enemy :
Receive it from me, then : war and confusion
In Cæsar's name pronounce I 'gainst thee : look
For fury, not to be resisted. Thus defied,
I thank thee for myself.

Cym.   Thou art welcome, Caius.
Thy Cæsar knighted me ; my youth I spent   70
Much under him ; of him I gather'd honour,
Which he, to seek of me again, perforce,
Behoves me keep at utterance. I am perfect
That the Pannonians and Dalmatians for
Their liberties are now in arms ; a precedent
Which not to read would show the Britons cold :
So Cæsar shall not find them.

Luc.   Let proof speak.

Clo. His majesty bids you welcome. Make pastime with

us a day, or two, or longer : if you seek us after-
wards in other terms, you shall find us in our salt-   80
water girdle : if you beat us out of it, it is yours ;
if you fall in the adventure, our crows shall fare the
better for you ; and there's an end.

Luc. So, sir.

Cym. I know your master's pleasure, and he mine :
   All the remain is ' Welcome.'   *Exeunt*

SCENE II

Another room in the palace

Enter Pisanio, with a letter

Pis. How ? of adultery ?   Wherefore write you not
   What monster's her accuser ?   Leonatus !
   O master, what a strange infection
   Is fall'n into thy ear ?   What false Italian,
   (As poisonous-tongued as handed) hath prevail'd
   On thy too ready hearing ?   Disloyal ?   No :
   She's punish'd for her truth ; and undergoes,
   More goddess-like than wife-like, such assaults
   As would take in some virtue.   O my master,
   Thy mind to her is now as low as were   10
   Thy fortunes.   How ? that I should murder her ?

Upon the love, and truth, and vows, which I
Have made to thy command? I, her? her blood?
If it be so to do good service, never
Let me be counted serviceable. How look I,
That I should seem to lack humanity
So much as this fact comes to? *(reading)* 'Do 't:
 the letter
That I have sent her, by her own command
Shall give thee opportunity.' O damn'd paper!
Black as the ink that's on thee! Senseless bauble, 20
Art thou a feodary for this act, and look'st
So virgin-like without? Lo, here she comes.
I am ignorant in what I am commanded.

Enter Imogen

Imo. How now, Pisanio?
Pis. Madam, here is a letter from my lord.
Imo. Who? thy lord? that is my lord Leonatus?
O, learn'd indeed were that astronomer
That knew the stars as I his characters;
He'ld lay the future open. You good gods,
Let what is here contain'd relish of love, 30
Of my lord's health, of his content, yet not
That we two are asunder; let that grieve him:
Some griefs are medicinable; that is one of them,

For it doth physic love : of his content,
All but in that !   Good wax, thy leave.   Blest be
You bees that make these locks of counsel !   Lovers
And men in dangerous bonds pray not alike :
Though forfeiters you cast in prison, yet
You clasp young Cupid's tables.   Good news, gods !
(*reads*) ' Justice, and your father's wrath (should he   40
take me in his dominion) could not be so cruel to me,
as you, O the dearest of creatures, would even renew
me with your eyes.   Take notice that I am in
Cambria, at Milford-Haven : what your own love
will out of this advise you, follow.   So he wishes
you all happiness, that remains loyal to his vow, and
your increasing in love,

                                 LEONATUS POSTHUMUS.'
O, for a horse with wings !   Hear'st thou, Pisanio ?
He is at Milford-Haven : read, and tell me   50
How far 'tis thither.   If one of mean affairs
May plod it in a week, why may not I
Glide thither in a day ?   Then, true Pisanio,—
Who long'st, like me, to see thy lord ; who long'st
(O, let me bate) but not like me ; yet long'st,
But in a fainter kind :—O, not like me ;
For mine 's beyond beyond : say, and speak thick,
(Love's counsellor should fill the bores of hearing,

To the smothering of the sense) how far it is
To this same blessed Milford : and by the way   60
Tell me how Wales was made so happy as
To inherit such a haven : but, first of all,
How we may steal from hence : and for the gap
That we shall make in time, from our hence-going
And our return, to excuse : but first, how get hence.
Why should excuse be born, or ere begot ?
We 'll talk of that hereafter.   Prithee, speak,
How many score of miles may we well ride
'Twixt hour and hour ?

Pis.   One score 'twixt sun and sun,
Madam, 's enough for you ; and too much too.   70

Imo. Why, one that rode to 's execution, man,
Could never go so slow : I have heard of riding
          wagers,
Where horses have been nimbler than the sands
That run i' the clock's behalf.   But this is foolery :
Go bid my woman feign a sickness, say
She 'll home to her father : and provide me presently
A riding-suit, no costlier than would fit
A franklin's housewife.

Pis.   Madam, you 're best consider.

Imo. I see before me, man : nor here, nor here,
Nor what ensues, but have a fog in them,   80

66

That I cannot look through.   Away, I prithee ;
Do as I bid thee : there 's no more to say ;
Accessible is none but Milford way.   *Exeunt*

SCENE III

Wales : a mountainous country with a cave

Enter Belarius, Guiderius, and Arviragus

Bel. **A** goodly day not to keep house with such
        Whose roof 's as low as ours !   Stoop, boys : this gate
        Instructs you how to adore the heavens, and bows you
        To a morning's holy office : the gates of monarchs
        Are arch'd so high that giants may jet through
        And keep their impious turbans on, without   †
        Good morrow to the sun.   Hail, thou fair heaven !
        We house i' the rock, yet use thee not so hardly
        As prouder livers do.

Gui.   Hail, heaven !

Arv.   Hail, heaven !

Bel. Now for our mountain sport : up to yond hill !   10
        Your legs are young : I 'll tread these flats.   Consider,
        When you above perceive me like a crow,
        That it is place which lessens and sets off :
        And you may then revolve what tales I have told you
        Of courts, of princes, of the tricks in war :

This service is not service, so being done,
But being so allow'd : to apprehend thus,
Draws us a profit from all things we see ;
And often, to our comfort, shall we find
The sharded beetle in a safer hold   20
Than is the full-wing'd eagle. O, this life
Is nobler than attending for a check,
Richer than doing nothing for a bauble,   †
Prouder than rustling in unpaid-for silk :
Such gain the cap of him that makes 'em fine,
Yet keeps his book uncross'd : no life to ours.

Gui. Out of your proof you speak : we, poor unfledg'd,
Have never wing'd from view o' the nest, nor know not
What air 's from home.   Haply this life is best
If quiet life be best, sweeter to you   30
That have a sharper known, well corresponding
With your stiff age : but unto us it is
A cell of ignorance, travelling a-bed,
A prison for a debtor that not dares
To stride a limit.

Arv.   What should we speak of
When we are old as you ? when we shall hear
The rain and wind beat dark December ? how
In this our pinching cave shall we discourse
The freezing hours away ? We have seen nothing :

We are beastly ; subtle as the fox for prey,   40
Like warlike as the wolf for what we eat :
Our valour is to chase what flies ; our cage
We make a quire, as doth the prison'd bird,
And sing our bondage freely.

Bel.   How you speak !
Did you but know the city's usuries,
And felt them knowingly : the art o' the court,
As hard to leave as keep ; whose top to climb
Is certain falling, or so slippery that
The fear 's as bad as falling : the toil o' the war,
A pain that only seems to seek out danger   50
I' the name of fame and honour, which dies i' the search,
And hath as oft a slanderous epitaph
As record of fair act ; nay, many times,
Doth ill deserve by doing well ; what 's worse,
Must court'sy at the censure :—O boys, this story
The world may read in me : my body 's mark'd
With Roman swords, and my report was once
First with the best of note : Cymbeline lov'd me,
And when a soldier was the theme, my name
Was not far off : then was I as a tree   60
Whose boughs did bend with fruit : but in one night,
A storm, or robbery (call it what you will)
Shook down my mellow hangings, nay, my leaves,

And left me bare to weather.

Gui.   Uncertain favour !

Bel. My fault being nothing (as I have told you oft)
But that two villains, whose false oaths prevail'd
Before my perfect honour, swore to Cymbeline
I was confederate with the Romans ; so
Follow'd my banishment, and this twenty years
This rock, and these demesnes, have been my world,   70
Where I have liv'd at honest freedom, paid
More pious debts to heaven than in all
The fore-end of my time.   But, up to the mountains ;
This is not hunters' language : he that strikes
The venison first shall be the lord o' the feast,
To him the other two shall minister,
And we will fear no poison, which attends
In place of greater state.   I 'll meet you in the valleys.

                        Exeunt Guiderius and Arviragus

How hard it is to hide the sparks of nature !
These boys know little they are sons to the king,   80
Nor Cymbeline dreams that they are alive.
They think they are mine, and though train'd up
        thus meanly
I' the cave wherein they bow, their thoughts do hit
The roofs of palaces, and nature prompts them
In simple and low things to prince it, much

Beyond the trick of others.   This Polydore,
The heir of Cymbeline and B. itain, who
The king his father call'd Guiderius,—Jove !
When on my three-foot stool I sit and tell
The warlike feats I have done, his spirits fly out   90
Into my story : say ' Thus mine enemy fell,
And thus I set my foot on 's neck,' even then
The princely blood flows in his cheek, he sweats,
Strains his young nerves, and puts himself in posture
That acts my words.   The younger brother, Cadwal,
Once Arviragus, in as like a figure
Strikes life into my speech, and shows much more
His own conceiving.   Hark, the game is rous'd !
O Cymbeline ! heaven and my conscience knows
Thou didst unjustly banish me : whereon,   100
At three and two years old, I stole these babes,
Thinking to bar thee of succession as
Thou reft'st me of my lands.   Euriphile,
Thou wast their nurse, they took thee for their mother,
And every day do honour to her grave :
Myself, Belarius, that am Morgan call'd,
They take for natural father.   The game is up.   *Exit*

SCENE IV

Country near Milford-Haven

Enter Pisanio and Imogen

Imo. Thou told'st me, when we came from horse, the place
　　　Was near at hand : ne'er long'd my mother so
　　　To see me first, as I have now.　Pisanio ! man !　　†
　　　Where is Posthumus ?　What is in thy mind,
　　　That makes thee stare thus ?　Wherefore breaks
　　　　　that sigh
　　　From the inward of thee ?　One but painted thus
　　　Would be interpreted a thing perplex'd
　　　Beyond self-explication : put thyself
　　　Into a haviour of less fear, ere wildness
　　　Vanquish my staider senses.　What 's the matter ?　10
　　　Why tender'st thou that paper to me, with
　　　A look untender ?　If 't be summer news,
　　　Smile to 't before ; if winterly, thou need'st
　　　But keep that countenance still.　My husband's hand ?
　　　That drug-damn'd Italy hath out-crafted him,
　　　And he 's at some hard point.　Speak, man, thy tongue
　　　May take off some extremity, which to read
　　　Would be even mortal to me.

Pis.　　　　　　　　　　　　Please you read,

And you shall find me, wretched man, a thing
The most disdain'd of fortune.   20

Imo. (*reads*) ' Thy mistress, Pisanio, hath play'd the
strumpet in my bed ; the testimonies whereof lies
bleeding in me.   I speak not out of weak surmises,
but from proof as strong as my grief, and as certain
as I expect my revenge.   That part thou, Pisanio,
must act for me, if thy faith be not tainted with the
breach of hers ; let thine own hands take away her
life : I shall give thee opportunity at Milford-Haven :
she hath my letter for the purpose ; where, if thou
fear to strike, and to make me certain it is done, thou   30
art the pandar to her dishonour, and equally to me
disloyal.'

Pis. What shall I need to draw my sword ? the paper
Hath cut her throat already.   No, 'tis slander,
Whose edge is sharper than the sword, whose tongue
Outvenoms all the worms of Nile, whose breath
Rides on the posting winds, and doth belie
All corners of the world : kings, queens, and states,
Maids, matrons, nay, the secrets of the grave,
This viperous slander enters.   What cheer, madam ?   40

Imo. False to his bed ?   What is it to be false ?
To lie in watch there, and to think on him ?
To weep 'twixt clock and clock ? if sleep charge nature,

73

To break it with a fearful dream of him,
And cry myself awake ? that 's false to 's bed, is it ?

Pis. Alas, good lady !

Imo. I false ?   Thy conscience witness : Iachimo,
Thou didst accuse him of incontinency ;
Thou then look'dst like a villain ; now, methinks,
Thy favour 's good enough.   Some jay of Italy,   50
Whose mother was her painting, hath betray'd him : †
Poor I am stale, a garment out of fashion,
And, for I am richer than to hang by the walls,
I must be ripp'd : to pieces with me : O,
Men's vows are women's traitors !   All good seeming,
By thy revolt, O husband, shall be thought
Put on for villany ; not born where 't grows,
But worn a bait for ladies.

Pis.   Good madam, hear me.

Imo. True honest men being heard, like false Æneas,   †
Were in his time thought false ; and Sinon's weeping 60
Did scandal many a holy tear, took pity
From most true wretchedness : so thou Posthumus,
Wilt lay the leaven on all proper men ;
Goodly, and gallant, shall be false and perjur'd
From thy great fail.   Come, fellow, be thou honest,
Do thou thy master's bidding.   When thou see'st him,
A little witness my obedience.   Look,

I draw the sword myself, take it, and hit
The innocent mansion of my love, my heart :
Fear not, 'tis empty of all things but grief :   70
Thy master is not there, who was indeed
The riches of it.   Do his bidding, strike,
Thou mayst be valiant in a better cause,
But now thou seem'st a coward.

Pis.   Hence, vile instrument,
Thou shalt not damn my hand.

Imo.   Why, I must die ;
And if I do not by thy hand, thou art
No servant of thy master's.   Against self-slaughter
There is a prohibition so divine
That cravens my weak hand.   Come, here's my
       heart ;—
Something 's afore 't.   Soft, soft ! we 'll no de- †
       fence ;—   80
Obedient as the scabbard.   What is here ?
The scriptures of the loyal Leonatus,
All turn'd to heresy ?   Away, away,
Corrupters of my faith, you shall no more
Be stomachers to my heart.   Thus may poor fools
Believe false teachers : though those that are betray'd
Do feel the treason sharply, yet the traitor
Stands in worse case of woe.

And thou, **Posthumus**, thou that didst set up
My disobedience 'gainst the king my father,   90
And make me put into contempt the suits
Of princely fellows, shalt hereafter find
It is no act of common passage, but
A strain of rareness : and I grieve myself
To think, when thou shalt be disedg'd by her
That now thou tirest on, how thy memory
Will then be pang'd by me.   Prithee dispatch :
The lamb entreats the butcher : where 's thy knife ?
Thou art too slow to do thy master's bidding,
When I desire it too.

Pis.   O gracious lady,   100
Since I receiv'd command to do this business
I have not slept one wink.

Imo.   Do 't, and to bed then.

Pis. I 'll wake mine eye-balls blind first.   †

Imo.   Wherefore then
Didst undertake it ?   Why hast thou abus'd
So many miles with a pretence ? this place ?
Mine action ? and thine own ? our horses' labour ?
The time inviting thee ? the perturb'd court,
For my being absent ? whereunto I never
Purpose return.   Why hast thou gone so far,
To be unbent when thou hast ta'en thy stand,   110

The elected deer before thee ?

Pis.   But to win time
To lose so bad employment, in the which
I have consider'd of a course.   Good lady,
Hear me with patience.

Imo.   Talk thy tongue weary, speak :
I have heard I am a strumpet, and mine ear,
Therein false struck, can take no greater wound,
Nor tent to bottom that.   But speak.

Pis.   Then, madam,
I thought you would not back again.

Imo.   Most like,
Bringing me here to kill me.

Pis.   Not so neither :
But if I were as wise as honest, then   120
My purpose would prove well.   It cannot be
But that my master is abus'd : some villain,
Ay, and singular in his art, hath done you both
This cursed injury.

Imo. Some Roman courtezan ?

Pis.   No, on my life :
I 'll give but notice you are dead, and send him
Some bloody sign of it ; for 'tis commanded
I should do so : you shall be miss'd at court,
And that will well confirm it.

Imo.   Why, good fellow,
  What shall I do the while ? where abide ? how live ? 130
  Or in my life what comfort, when I am
  Dead to my husband ?

Pis.   If you 'll back to the court—

Imo. No court, no father, nor no more ado
  With that harsh, noble, simple nothing,   †
  That Cloten, whose love-suit hath been to me
  As fearful as a siege.

Pis.   If not at court,
  Then not in Britain must you bide.

Imo.   Where then ?
  Hath Britain all the sun that shines ?   Day ? night ?
  Are they not but in Britain ?   I' the world's volume
  Our Britain seems as of it, but not in 't ;   140
  In a great pool a swan's nest : prithee think
  There 's livers out of Britain.

Pis.   I am most glad
  You think of other place.   The ambassador,
  Lucius the Roman, comes to Milford-Haven
  To-morrow : now, if you could wear a mind
  Dark, as your fortune is, and but disguise
  That which, to appear itself, must not yet be,
  But by self-danger, you should tread a course
  Pretty, and full of view ; yea, haply, near

The residence of Posthumus ; so nigh at least   150
That though his actions were not visible, yet
Report should render him hourly to your ear
As truly as he moves.

Imo.   O for such means,
Though peril to my modesty, not death on 't,
I would adventure !

Pis.   Well then, here 's the point :
You must forget to be a woman ; change
Command into obedience ; fear and niceness
(The handmaids of all women, or, more truly,
Woman it pretty self) into a waggish courage ;
Ready in gibes, quick-answer'd, saucy, and   160
As quarrelous as the weasel ; nay, you must
Forget that rarest treasure of your cheek,
Exposing it (but, O, the harder heart !
Alack, no remedy !) to the greedy touch
Of common-kissing Titan, and forget
Your laboursome and dainty trims, wherein
You made great Juno angry.

Imo.   Nay, be brief :
I see into thy end, and am almost
A man already.

Pis.   First, make yourself but like one.
Fore-thinking this, I have already fit   170

    ('Tis in my cloak-bag) doublet, hat, hose, all
    That answer to them : would you, in their serving
    (And with what imitation you can borrow
    From youth of such a season) 'fore noble Lucius
    Present yourself, desire his service, tell him
    Wherein you're happy,—which you'll make him
        know,
    If that his head have ear in music,—doubtless
    With joy he will embrace you ; for he's honourable,
    And, doubling that, most holy.   Your means abroad,
    You have me, rich ; and I will never fail   180
    Beginning nor supplyment.

Imo.   Thou art all the comfort
    The gods will diet me with.   Prithee, away :
    There's more to be consider'd ; but we'll even
    All that good time will give us : this attempt
    I am soldier to, and will abide it with
    A prince's courage.   Away, I prithee.

Pis. Well, madam, we must take a short farewell,
    Lest, being miss'd, I be suspected of
    Your carriage from the court.   My noble mistress,
    Here is a box ; I had it from the queen :   190
    What's in't is precious ; if you are sick at sea,
    Or stomach-qualm'd at land, a dram of this
    Will drive away distemper.   To some shade,

And fit you to your manhood : may the gods
Direct you to the best ;

Imo. Amen : I thank thee.   *Exeunt severally*

SCENE V

A room in Cymbeline's palace

Enter Cymbeline, Queen, Cloten, Lucius, and Lords

*Cym.*Thus far, and so farewell.
Luc. Thanks, royal sir.
My emperor hath wrote, I must from hence,
And am right sorry that I must report ye
My master's enemy.
Cym. Our subjects, sir,
Will not endure his yoke ; and for ourself
To show less sovereignty than they, must needs
Appear unkinglike.
Luc. So, sir : I desire of you
A conduct over-land to Milford-Haven.
Madam, all joy befal your grace, and you !
*Cym.*My lords, you are appointed for that office ;   10
The due of honour in no point omit.
So farewell, noble Lucius.
Luc. Your hand, my lord.

Clo. Receive it friendly ; but from this time forth
   I wear it as your enemy.

Luc.   Sir, the event
   Is yet to name the winner : fare you well.

Cym. Leave not the worthy Lucius, good my lords,
   Till he have cross'd the Severn.   Happiness !

                         Exeunt Lucius and Lords

Qu. He goes hence frowning : but it honours us
   That we have given him cause.

Clo.   'Tis all the better ;
   Your valiant Britons have their wishes in it.   20

Cym. Lucius hath wrote already to the emperor
   How it goes here.   It fits us therefore ripely
   Our chariots and our horsemen be in readiness :
   The powers that he already hath in Gallia
   Will soon be drawn to head, from whence he moves
   His war for Britain.

Qu.   'Tis not sleepy business,
   But must be look'd to speedily, and strongly.

Cym. Our expectation that it would be thus
   Hath made us forward.   But, my gentle queen,
   Where is our daughter ?   She hath not appear'd   30
   Before the Roman, nor to us hath tender'd
   The duty of the day : she looks us like
   A thing more made of malice than of duty ;

We have noted it.   Call her before us, for
We have been too slight in sufferance.

Exit an Attendant

Qu.   Royal sir,
Since the exile of Posthumus, most retir'd
Hath her life been ; the cure whereof, my lord,
'Tis time must do.   Beseech your majesty,
Forbear sharp speeches to her : she 's a lady
So tender of rebukes that words are strokes,   40
And strokes death to her.

Re-enter Attendant

Cym.   Where is she, sir ?   How
Can her contempt be answer'd ?

Atten.   Please you, sir,
Her chambers are all lock'd, and there 's no answer
That will be given to the loud'st of noise we make.

Qu. My lord, when last I went to visit her,
She pray'd me to excuse her keeping close,
Whereto constrain'd by her infirmity,
She should that duty leave unpaid to you,
Which daily she was bound to proffer : this
She wish'd me to make known ; but our great court   50
Made me to blame in memory.

Cym.   Her doors lock'd ?
Not seen of late ?   Grant heavens, that which I fear

      Prove false!   *Exit*

Qu. Son, I say, follow the king.

Clo. That man of hers, Pisanio, her old servant,
    I have not seen these two days.

Qu.   Go, look after.

                            Exit Cloten

    Pisanio, thou that stand'st so for Posthumus!
    He hath a drug of mine; I pray his absence
    Proceed by swallowing that; for he believes
    It is a thing most precious. But for her,   60
    Where is she gone? Haply, despair hath seiz'd her;
    Or, wing'd with fervour of her love, she's flown
    To her desir'd Posthumus: gone she is
    To death, or to dishonour, and my end
    Can make good use of either: she being down,
    I have the placing of the British crown.

                     Re-enter Cloten

    How now, my son?

Clo.   'Tis certain she is fled:
    Go in and cheer the king, he rages, none
    Dare come about him.

Qu.   *(aside)* All the better: may
    This night forestall him of the coming day!   *Exit* 70

Clo. I love and hate her: for she's fair and royal,
    And that she hath **all** courtly parts more exquisite

Than lady, ladies, woman, from every one
The best she hath, and she, of all compounded,
Outsells them all ; I love her therefore, but
Disdaining me, and throwing favours on
The low Posthumus, slanders so her judgement
That what's else rare is chok'd ; and in that point
I will conclude to hate her, nay, indeed,
To be reveng'd upon her.   For when fools   80
Shall—

Enter Pisanio

       Who is here ?   What, are you packing, sirrah ?
Come hither ! ah, you precious pandar, villain,
Where is thy lady ?   In a word, or else
Thou art straightway with the fiends.

Pis.   O, good my lord !

Clo. Where is thy lady ? or, by Jupiter,—
I will not ask again.   Close villain,
I 'll have this secret from thy heart, or rip
Thy heart to find it.   Is she with Posthumus ?
From whose so many weights of baseness cannot
A dram of worth be drawn.

Pis.   Alas, my lord,   90
How can she be with him ?   When was she miss'd ?
He is in Rome.

Clo.   Where is she, sir ?   Come nearer ;

No farther halting : satisfy me home,
What is become of her ?

Pis. O, my all-worthy lord !

Clo.   All-worthy villain !
Discover where thy mistress is, at once,
At the next word : no more of ' worthy lord ! '
Speak, or thy silence on the instant is
Thy condemnation and thy death.

Pis.   Then, sir,
This paper is the history of my knowledge   100
Touching her flight.   *Presenting a letter*

Clo.   Let 's see 't.   I will pursue her
Even to Augustus' throne.

Pis.   (*aside*) Or this, or perish.
She 's far enough ; and what he learns by this
May prove his travel, not her danger.

Clo.   Hum !

Pis. (*aside*) I 'll write to my lord she 's dead. O Imogen,
Safe mayst thou wander, safe return again !

Clo. Sirrah, is this letter true ?

Pis. Sir, as I think.

Clo. It is Posthumus' hand, I know 't. Sirrah, if thou
wouldst not be a villain, but do me true service, 110
undergo those employments wherein I should have
cause to use thee with a serious industry, that is,

what villany soe'er I bid thee do, to perform it
directly and truly, I would think thee an honest man :
thou shouldst neither want my means for thy relief,
nor my voice for thy preferment.

Pis. Well, my good lord.

Clo. Wilt thou serve me ? for since patiently and con-
stantly thou hast stuck to the bare fortune of that
beggar Posthumus, thou canst not, in the course of 120
gratitude, but be a diligent follower of mine.   Wilt
thou serve me ?

Pis. Sir, I will.

Clo. Give me thy hand, here's my purse.   Hast any of
thy late master's garments in thy possession ?

Pis. I have, my lord, at my lodging, the same suit he
wore when he took leave of my lady and mistress.

Clo. The first service thou dost me, fetch that suit hither,
let it be thy first service, go.

Pis. I shall, my lord.   *Exit* 130

Clo. Meet thee at Milford-Haven ! (I forgot to ask him
one thing ; I'll remember't anon :) even there,
thou villain Posthumus, will I kill thee.   I would
these garments were come.   She said upon a time
(the bitterness of it I now belch from my heart) that
she held the very garment of Posthumus in more
respect than my noble and natural person, together

with the adornment of my qualities. With that
suit upon my back, will I ravish her: first kill him,
and in her eyes; there shall she see my valour, 140
which will then be a torment to her contempt. He
on the ground, my speech of insultment ended on
his dead body, and when my lust hath dined (which,
as I say, to vex her I will execute in the clothes that
she so prais'd) to the court I'll knock her back,
foot her home again. She hath despis'd me re-
joicingly, and I'll be merry in my revenge.

Re-enter Pisanio, with the clothes

Be those the garments?

Pis. Ay, my noble lord.

Clo. How long is't since she went to Milford-Haven? 150

Pis. She can scarce be there yet.

Clo. Bring this apparel to my chamber, that is the second
thing that I have commanded thee: the third is,
that thou wilt be a voluntary mute to my design.
Be but duteous, and true preferment shall tender
itself to thee. My revenge is now at Milford,
would I had wings to follow it! Come, and be
true.   *Exit*

Pis. Thou bid'st me to my loss: for, true to thee
Were to prove false, which I will never be,   160
To him that is most true. To Milford go,

And find not her whom thou pursuest.   Flow, flow,
You heavenly blessings, on her !   This fool's speed
Be cross'd with slowness ; labour be his meed !

Exit

SCENE VI

Wales : before the cave of Belarius

Enter Imogen, in boy's clothes

Imo. I see a man's life is a tedious one :
I have tir'd myself ; and for two nights together
Have made the ground my bed.   I should be sick,
But that my resolution helps me.   Milford,
When from the mountain-top Pisanio show'd thee,
Thou wast within a ken : O Jove ! I think
Foundations fly the wretched ; such, I mean,
Where they should be reliev'd.   Two beggars told me
I could not miss my way : will poor folks lie,
That have afflictions on them, knowing 'tis   10
A punishment or trial ?   Yes ; no wonder,
When rich ones scarce tell true : to lapse in fulness
Is sorer than to lie for need ; and falsehood
Is worse in kings than beggars.   My dear lord !
Thou art one o' the false ones : now I think on thee,
My hunger 's gone ; but even before, I was

At point to sink for food.   But what is this?
Here is a path to 't: 'tis some savage hold:
I were best not call; I dare not call: yet famine,
Ere clean it o'erthrow nature, makes it valiant.   20
Plenty and peace breeds cowards; hardness ever
Of hardiness is mother.   Ho! who's here?
If any thing that's civil, speak; if savage,
Take, or lend.   Ho!   No answer?   then I'll enter.
Best draw my sword; and if mine enemy
But fear the sword like me, he'll scarcely look on 't.
Such a foe, good heavens!   *Exit, to the cave*
          Enter Belarius, Guiderius, and Arviragus

Bel. You, Polydore, have prov'd best woodman, and
          Are master of the feast: Cadwal and I
          Will play the cook, and servant; 'tis our match: 30
          The sweat and industry would dry, and die,
          But for the end it works to.   Come, our stomachs
          Will make what's homely savoury: weariness
          Can snore upon the flint, when resty sloth
          Finds the down pillow hard.   Now, peace be here,
          Poor house, that keep'st thyself!

Gui.   I am throughly weary.
Arv. I am weak with toil, yet strong in appetite.
Gui. There is cold meat i' the cave, we'll browse on that,
          Whilst what we have kill'd be cook'd.

Bel.   (*looking into the cave*) Stay, come not in :
          But that it eats our victuals, I should think   40
          Here were a fairy.

Gui.   What 's the matter, sir ?

Bel. By Jupiter, an angel ! or, if not,
          An earthly paragon !   Behold divineness
          No elder than a boy !

                    Re-enter Imogen

Imo. Good masters, harm me not :
          Before I enter'd here, I call'd, and thought
          To have begg'd, or bought, what I have took : good
               troth,
          I have stol'n nought, nor would not, though I had
               found
          Gold strew'd i' the floor.   Here 's money for my meat,
          I would have left it on the board, so soon   50
          As I had made my meal, and parted
          With prayers for the provider.

Gui.   Money, youth ?

Arv. All gold and silver rather turn to dirt,
          As 'tis no better reckon'd, but of those
          Who worship dirty gods.

Imo.   I see you 're angry :
          Know, if you kill me for my fault, I should
          Have died had I not made it.

Bel.   Whither bound ?

Imo. To Milford-Haven.

Bel. What 's your name ?

Imo. Fidele, sir.   I have a kinsman, who   60
    Is bound for Italy ; he embark'd at Milford ;
    To whom being going, almost spent with hunger,
    I am fall'n in this offence.

Bel.   Prithee, fair youth,
    Think us no churls ; nor measure our good minds
    By this rude place we live in.   Well encounter'd !
    'Tis almost night, you shall have better cheer
    Ere you depart : and thanks to stay and eat it.
    Boys, bid him welcome.

Gui.   Were you a woman, youth,
    I should woo hard but be your groom in honesty :   †
    I bid for you as I 'ld buy.

Arv.   I 'll make 't my comfort   70
    He is a man, I 'll love him as my brother :
    And such a welcome as I 'ld give to him
    After long absence, such is yours : most welcome !
    Be sprightly, for you fall 'mongst friends.

Imo   'Mongst friends,
    If brothers.   (*aside*) Would it had been so, that they
    Had been my father's sons ! then had my prize   †
    Been less, and so more equal ballasting

    To thee, Posthumus.

Bel.   He wrings at some distress.

Gui. Would I could free 't !

Arv.   Or I, whate'er it be,

    What pain it cost, what danger !   Gods !

Bel.   Hark, boys.   80

                        Whispering

Imo. Great men,

    That had a court no bigger than this cave,

    That did attend themselves, and had the virtue

    Which their own conscience seal'd them—laying by

    That nothing-gift of differing multitudes—

    Could not out-peer these twain.   Pardon me, gods !

    I 'll change my sex to be companion with them,

    Since Leonatus' false.

Bel.   It shall be so :

    Boys, we 'll go dress our hunt.   Fair youth, come in :

    Discourse is heavy, fasting ; when we have supp'd,   90

    We 'll mannerly demand thee of thy story,

    So far as thou wilt speak it.

Gui.   Pray, draw near.

Arv. The night to the owl and morn to the lark less
       welcome.

Imo. Thanks, sir.

Arv. I pray, draw near.   *Exeunt*

SCENE VII

Rome.   A public place

Enter two Senators and Tribunes

1.*S.* This is the tenour of the emperor's writ :
     That since the common men are now in action
     'Gainst the Pannonians and Dalmatians,
     And that the legions now in Gallia are
     Full weak to undertake our wars against
     The fall'n-off Britons, that we do incite
     The gentry to this business.   He creates
     Lucius proconsul : and to you the tribunes,
     For this immediate levy, he commends
     His absolute commission.   Long live Cæsar !   10
1.*T.* Is Lucius general of the forces ?
2.*S.*   Ay.
1.*T.* Remaining now in Gallia ?
1.*S.*   With those legions
     Which I have spoke of, whereunto your levy
     Must be suppliant : the words of your commission
     Will tie you to the numbers, and the time
     Of their dispatch.
1.*T.*   We will discharge our duty. *Exeunt*

Act Fourth

SCENE I

Wales : near the cave of Belarius

Enter Cloten alone

Clo. I am near to the place where they should meet, if
Pisanio have mapp'd it truly. How fit his garments
serve me ! Why should his mistress, who was made
by him that made the tailor, not be fit too ? the rather
(saving reverence of the word) for 'tis said a woman's
fitness comes by fits. Therein I must play the work-
man. I dare speak it to myself, for it is not vain-
glory for a man and his glass to confer in his own
chamber ; I mean, the lines of my body are as well
drawn as his ; no less young, more strong, not   10
beneath him in fortunes, beyond him in the advantage of the time, above him in birth, alike conversant
in general services, and more remarkable in single
oppositions ; yet this imperseverant thing loves   †
him in my despite. What mortality is ! Posthumus,
thy head (which now is growing upon thy shoulders)
shall within this hour be off, thy mistress enforc'd,

thy garments cut to pieces before thy face : and all
this done, spurn her home to her father ; who may
haply be a little angry for my so rough usage ; but   20
my mother, having power of his testiness, shall turn
all into my commendations. My horse is tied up
safe : out, sword, and to a sore purpose ! Fortune
put them into my hand ! This is the very description
of their meeting-place, and the fellow dares not
deceive me.   *Exit*

SCENE II

Before the cave of Belarius

*Enter, from the cave, Belarius, Guiderius, Arviragus,
and Imogen*

Bel. (*to Imogen*) You are not well : remain here in the cave,
    We 'll come to you after hunting.

Arv.   (*to Imogen*) Brother, stay here :
    Are we not brothers ?

Imo.   So man and man should be,
    But clay and clay differs in dignity,
    Whose dust is both alike.   I am very sick.

Gui. Go you to hunting, I 'll abide with him.

Imo. So sick I am not, yet I am not well ;
    But not so citizen a wanton as

To seem to die ere sick : so please you, leave me,
Stick to your journal course : the breach of custom   10
Is breach of all.   I am ill, but your being by me
Cannot amend me : society is no comfort
To one not sociable : I am not very sick,
Since I can reason of it.   Pray you, trust me here :
I 'll rob none but myself, and let me die,
Stealing so poorly.

Gui.   I love thee ; I have spoke it,
How much the quantity, the weight as much,
As I do love my father.

Bel.   What ? how ? how ?

Arv. If it be sin to say so, sir, I yoke me
In my good brother's fault : I know not why   20
I love this youth, and I have heard you say,
Love's reason 's without reason : the bier at door,
And a demand who is 't shall die, I 'ld say
' My father, not this youth.'

Bel.   (*aside*) O noble strain !
O worthiness of nature, breed of greatness !
Cowards father cowards and base things sire base :
Nature hath meal and bran, contempt and grace.
I 'm not their father, yet who this should be,
Doth miracle itself, lov'd before me.—
'Tis the ninth hour o' the morn.

Arv.   Brother, farewell.   30

Imo. I wish ye sport.

Arv.   You health.   So please you, sir.

Imo. (*aside*) These are kind creatures.   Gods, what lies I
                have heard !
        Our courtiers say all 's savage but at court :
        Experience, O, thou disprov'st report !
        The imperious seas breed monsters ; for the dish,
        Poor tributary rivers as sweet fish.
        I am sick still, heart-sick.   Pisanio,
        I 'll now taste of thy drug.   *Swallows some*

Gui.   I could not stir him :
        He said he was gentle, but unfortunate ;
        Dishonestly afflicted, but yet honest.   40

Arv. Thus did he answer me : yet said, hereafter
        I might know more.

Bel.   To the field, to the field !
        We 'll leave you for this time : go in and rest.

Arv. We 'll not be long away.

Bel.   Pray, be not sick,
        For you must be our housewife.

Imo.   Well, or ill,
        I am bound to you.

Bel.   And shalt be ever.

                            Exit Imogen, to the cave

                            98

This youth, howe'er distress'd, appears he hath had
Good ancestors.

Arv.   How angel-like he sings !

Gui. But his neat cookery ! he cut our roots
In characters ;   50
And sauc'd our broths, as Juno had been sick,
And he her dieter.

Arv.   Nobly he yokes
A smiling with a sigh ; as if the sigh
Was that it was, for not being such a smile ;
The smile, mocking the sigh, that it would fly
From so divine a temple, to commix
With winds that sailors rail at.

Gui.   I do note
That grief and patience, rooted in him both,
Mingle their spurs together.

Arv.   Grow, patience !
And let the stinking elder, grief, untwine   60
His perishing root with the increasing vine !

Bel. It is great morning.   Come, away !—Who 's there ?

Enter Cloten

Clo. I cannot find those runagates, that villain
Hath mock'd me : I am faint.

Bel.   ' Those runagates ! '
Means he not us ?   I partly know him, 'tis

Cloten, the son o' the queen. I fear some ambush.
I saw him not these many years, and yet
I know 'tis he. We are held as outlaws : hence !

Gui. He is but one : you and my brother search
What companies are near : pray you, away ;
Let me alone with him.   70

                         Exeunt Belarius and Arviragus

Clo.   Soft, what are you
That fly me thus ? some villain mountaineers ?
I have heard of such. What slave art thou ?

Gui.   A thing
More slavish did I ne'er than answering
A slave without a knock.

Clo.   Thou art a robber,
A law-breaker, a villain : yield thee, thief.

Gui. To who ? to thee ? What art thou ? Have not I
An arm as big as thine ? a heart as big ?
Thy words, I grant, are bigger ; for I wear not
My dagger in my mouth. Say what thou art,   80
Why I should yield to thee.

Clo.   Thou villain base,
Know'st me not by my clothes ?

Gui.   No, nor thy tailor, rascal ;
Who is thy grandfather ? he made those clothes,
Which, as it seems, make thee.

Clo.   Thou precious varlet,
     My tailor made them not.
Gui.   Hence then, and thank
     The man that gave them thee. Thou art some fool;
     I am loath to beat thee.
Clo.   Thou injurious thief,
     Hear but my name, and tremble.
Gui.   What's thy name?
Clo. Cloten, thou villain.
Gui. Cloten, thou double villain, be thy name,   90
     I cannot tremble at it: were it Toad, or Adder, Spider,
     'Twould move me sooner.
Clo.   To thy further fear,
     Nay, to thy mere confusion, thou shalt know
     I am son to the queen.
Gui.   I am sorry for't; not seeming
     So worthy as thy birth.
Clo.   Art not afeard?
Gui. Those that I reverence, those I fear; the wise;
     At fools I laugh, not fear them.
Clo.   Die the death:
     When I have slain thee with my proper hand,
     I'll follow those that even now fled hence,
     And on the gates of Lud's town set your heads: 100
     Yield, rustic mountaineer.   *Exeunt fighting*

Re-enter Belarius and Arviragus

Bel. No companies abroad ?

Arv. None in the world : you did mistake him, sure.

Bel. I cannot tell : long is it since I saw him,
But time hath nothing blurr'd those lines of favour
Which then he wore ; the snatches in his voice,
And burst of speaking, were as his : I am absolute
'Twas very Cloten.

Arv.   In this place we left them :
I wish my brother make good time with him,
You say he is so fell.

Bel.   Being scarce made up,   110
I mean, to man, he had not apprehension
Of roaring terrors : for defect of judgement
Is oft the cause of fear.   But see, thy brother.

Re-enter Guiderius with Cloten's head

Gui. This Cloten was a fool, an empty purse,
There was no money in 't : not Hercules
Could have knock'd out his brains, for he had none :
Yet I not doing this, the fool had borne
My head, as I do his.

Bel.   What hast thou done ?

Gui. I am perfect what : cut off one Cloten's head,
Son to the queen (after his own report)   120
Who call'd me traitor, mountaineer, and swore,

       With his own single hand he 'ld take us in,
       Displace our heads where (thank the gods !) they grow,
       And set them on Lud's town.

Bel.   We are all undone.

Gui. Why, worthy father, what have we to lose,
       But that he swore to take, our lives ?   The law
       Protects not us : then why should we be tender
       To let an arrogant piece of flesh threat us,
       Play judge and executioner, all himself,
       For we do fear the law ?   What company   130
       Discover you abroad ?

Bel.   No single soul
       Can we set eye on ; but in all safe reason
       He must have some attendants.   Though his humour
       Was nothing but mutation, ay, and that
       From one bad thing to worse, not frenzy, not
       Absolute madness could so far have rav'd,
       To bring him here alone : although perhaps
       It may be heard at court that such as we
       Cave here, hunt here, are outlaws, and in time
       May make some stronger head, the which he hearing 140
       (As it is like him) might break out, and swear
       He 'ld fetch us in, yet is 't not probable
       To come alone, either he so undertaking,
       Or they so suffering : then on good ground we fear,

  If we do fear this body hath a tail
  More perilous than the head.

Arv.   Let ordinance
  Come as the gods foresay it : howsoe'er,
  My brother hath done well.

Bel.   I had no mind
  To hunt this day : the boy Fidele's sickness
  Did make my way long forth.

Gui.   With his own sword,   150
  Which he did wave against my throat, I have ta'en
  His head from him : I 'll throw 't into the creek
  Behind our rock, and let it to the sea,
  And tell the fishes he 's the queen's son, Cloten :
  That 's all I reck.   *Exit*

Bel.   I fear 'twill be reveng'd :
  Would, Polydore, thou hadst not done 't ! though
    valour
  Becomes thee well enough.

Arv.   Would I had done 't,
  So the revenge alone pursued me ! Polydore,
  I love thee brotherly, but envy much
  Thou hast robb'd me of this deed : I would revenges,   160
  That possible strength might meet, would seek us
    through
  And put us to our answer.

Bel.   Well, 'tis done :
We 'll hunt no more to-day, nor seek for danger
Where there 's no profit.   I prithee to our rock ;
You and Fidele play the cooks : I 'll stay
Till hasty Polydore return, and bring him
To dinner presently.

Arv.   Poor sick Fidele !
I 'll willingly to him : to gain his colour
I 'ld let a parish of such Clotens blood,
And praise myself for charity.   *Exit*

Bel.   O thou goddess,   170
Thou divine Nature, thou thyself thou blazon'st
In these two princely boys !   They are as gentle
As zephyrs blowing below the violet,
Not wagging his sweet head ; and yet, as rough
(Their royal blood enchaf'd) as the rud'st wind,
That by the top doth take the mountain pine,
And make him stoop to the vale.   'Tis wonder
That an invisible instinct should frame them
To royalty unlearn'd, honour untaught,
Civility not seen from other, valour   180
That wildly grows in them, but yields a crop
As if it had been sow'd.   Yet still it 's strange
What Cloten's being here to us portends,
Or what his death will bring us.

Re-enter Guiderius

Gui.   Where's my brother?
I have sent Cloten's clotpoll down the stream,
In embassy to his mother: his body's hostage
For his return.   *Solemn music*

Bel.   My ingenious instrument!
Hark, Polydore, it sounds! But what occasion
Hath Cadwal now to give it motion? Hark!

Gui. Is he at home?

Bel.   He went hence even now.   190

Gui. What does he mean? Since death of my dear'st
          mother
It did not speak before. All solemn things
Should answer solemn accidents. The matter?
Triumphs for nothing and lamenting toys
Is jollity for apes and grief for boys.
Is Cadwal mad?

*Re-enter Arviragus with Imogen, as dead, bearing
her in his arms*

Bel.   Look, here he comes,
And brings the dire occasion in his arms
Of what we blame him for!

Arv.   The bird is dead
That we have made so much on. I had rather
Have skipp'd from sixteen years of age to sixty,   200

To have turn'd my leaping-time into a crutch,
Than have seen this.

Gui.   O sweetest, fairest lily !
My brother wears thee not one half so well
As when thou grew'st thyself.

Bel.   O melancholy !
Who ever yet could sound thy bottom ? find
The ooze, to show what coast thy sluggish crare   †
Might easiest harbour in ?   Thou blessed thing !   †
Jove knows what man thou mightst have made ; but I,
Thou diedst, a most rare boy, of melancholy.
How found you him ?

Arv.   Stark, as you see :   210
Thus smiling, as some fly had tickled slumber,
Not as death's dart being laugh'd at ; his right cheek
Reposing on a cushion.

Gui.   Where ?

Arv.   O' the floor ;
His arms thus leagu'd, I thought he slept, and put
My clouted brogues from off my feet, whose rudeness
Answer'd my steps too loud.

Gui.   Why, he but sleeps :
If he be gone, he 'll make his grave a bed ;
With female fairies will his tomb be haunted,
And worms will not come to thee.

Arv.   With fairest flowers,
Whilst summer lasts, and I live here, Fidele,   220
I 'll sweeten thy sad grave : thou shalt not lack
The flower that 's like thy face, pale primrose, nor
The azur'd harebell, like thy veins ; no, nor
The leaf of eglantine, whom not to slander,
Out-sweeten'd not thy breath : the ruddock would
With charitable bill (O bill, sore shaming
Those rich-left heirs that let their fathers lie
Without a monument) bring thee all this,
Yea, and furr'd moss besides, when flowers are none,
To winter-ground thy corse.

Gui.   Prithee, have done,   230
And do not play in wench-like words with that
Which is so serious.   Let us bury him,
And not protract with admiration what
Is now due debt.   To the grave.

Arv.   Say, where shall 's lay him ?

Gui. By good Euriphile, our mother.

Arv.   Be 't so :
And let us, Polydore, though now our voices
Have got the mannish crack, sing him to the ground,
As once our mother ; use like note, and words,
Save that ' Euriphile ' must be ' Fidele.'

Gui. Cadwal,   240

    I cannot sing : I 'll weep, and word it with thee ;
    For notes of sorrow, out of tune, are worse
    Than priests and fanes that lie.

Arv.   We 'll speak it then.

Bel. Great griefs, I see, medicine the less ; for Cloten
    Is quite forgot. He was a queen's son, boys,
    And though he came our enemy, remember
    He was paid for that : though mean and mighty, rotting
    Together, have one dust, yet reverence
    (That angel of the world) doth make distinction
    Of place 'tween high and low. Our foe was princely, **250**
    And though you took his life, as being our foe,
    Yet bury him as a prince.

Gui.   Pray you, fetch him hither,
    Thersites' body is as good as Ajax',
    When neither are alive.

Arv.   If you 'll go fetch him,
    We 'll say our song the whilst. Brother, begin.

                                   Exit Belarius

Gui. Nay, Cadwal, we must lay his head to the east,
    My father hath a reason for 't.

Arv.   'Tis true.

Gui. Come on then, and remove him.

Arv.   So. Begin.

SONG

Gui.	Fear no more the heat o' the sun,	
	Nor the furious winter's rages,	260
	Thou thy worldly task hast done,	
	Home art gone, and ta'en thy wages :	
	Golden lads and girls all must,	
	As chimney-sweepers, come to dust.	

Arv.	Fear no more the frown o' the great,
	Thou art past the tyrant's stroke,
	Care no more to clothe and eat,
	To thee the reed is as the oak :
	The sceptre, learning, physic, must
	All follow this and come to dust. 270

Gui.	Fear no more the lightning-flash ;
Arv.	Nor the all-dreaded thunder-stone ;
Gui.	Fear not slander, censure rash ;
Arv.	Thou hast finish'd joy and moan :
Both.	All lovers young, all lovers must
	Consign to thee and come to dust.

Gui.	No exorciser harm thee !	
Arv.	Nor no witchcraft charm thee !	
Gui.	Ghost unlaid forbear thee !	
Arv.	Nothing ill come near thee !	280

Both.   Quiet consummation have,
         And renowned be thy grave!

Re-enter Belarius with the body of Cloten

Gui. We have done our obsequies: come, lay him down.
Bel. Here's a few flowers, but 'bout midnight more:
      The herbs that have on them cold dew o' the night
      Are strewings fitt'st for graves.   Upon their faces.
      You were as flowers, now wither'd: even so
      These herblets shall, which we upon you strow.
      Come on, away, apart upon our knees.
      The ground that gave them first has them again: 290
      Their pleasures here are past, so is their pain.

      Exeunt Belarius, Guiderius, and Arviragus

Imo. (*awaking*) Yes, sir, to Milford-Haven, which is the
            way?—
      I thank you.—By yond bush?—Pray, how far thither?
      'Ods pittikins! can it be six mile yet?—
      I have gone all night:—faith, I'll lie down and sleep.
      But, soft! no bedfellow?   O gods and goddesses!

            Seeing the body of Cloten

      These flowers are like the pleasures of the world;
      This bloody man, the care on't.   I hope I dream;
      For so I thought I was a cave-keeper,
      And cook to honest creatures: but 'tis not so;   300

111

'Twas but a bolt of nothing, shot at nothing,
Which the brain makes of fumes : our very eyes
Are sometimes like our judgements, blind.   Good
    faith,
I tremble still with fear : but if there be
Yet left in heaven as small a drop of pity
As a wren's eye, fear'd gods, a part of it !
The dream's here still : even when I wake, it is
Without me, as within me ; not imagin'd, felt.
A headless man ?   The garments of Posthumus ?
I know the shape of 's leg : this is his hand ;   310
His foot Mercurial ; his Martial thigh,
The brawns of Hercules : but his Jovial face—
Murder in heaven ?—How ?—'Tis gone.   Pisanio,
All curses madded Hecuba gave the Greeks,
And mine to boot, be darted on thee !   Thou,
Conspir'd with that irregulous devil, Cloten,
Hast here cut off my lord.   To write and read
Be henceforth treacherous !   Damn'd Pisanio
Hath with his forged letters (damn'd Pisanio)
From this most bravest vessel of the world   320
Struck the main-top !   O Posthumus, alas,
Where is thy head ? where's that ?   Ay me ! where's
    that ?
Pisanio might have kill'd thee at the heart,

And left this head on.   How should this be, Pisanio?
'Tis he, and Cloten: malice and lucre in them
Have laid this woe here.   O, 'tis pregnant, pregnant!
The drug he gave me, which he said was precious
And cordial to me, have I not found it
Murderous to the senses?   That confirms it home:
This is Pisanio's deed, and Cloten's: O!   330
Give colour to my pale cheek with thy blood,
That we the horrider may seem to those
Which chance to find us: O, my lord, my lord!

> *Falls on the body*
> *Enter Lucius, a Captain and other Officers, and*
> *a Soothsayer*

Cap. To them, the legions garrison'd in Gallia
After your will have cross'd the sea, attending
You here at Milford-Haven with your ships:
They are here in readiness.

Luc.   But what from Rome?

Cap. The senate hath stirr'd up the confiners
And gentlemen of Italy, most willing spirits
That promise noble service: and they come   340
Under the conduct of bold Iachimo,
Syenna's brother.

Luc.   When expect you them?

Cap. With the next benefit o' the wind.

Luc.   This forwardness
    Makes our hopes fair. Command our present numbers
    Be muster'd ; bid the captains look to 't. Now, sir,
    What have you dream'd of late of this war's purpose ?

Sooth. Last night the very gods show'd me a vision
    (I fast and pray'd for their intelligence) thus :
    I saw Jove's bird, the Roman eagle, wing'd
    From the spongy south to this part of the west,   350
    There vanish'd in the sunbeams, which portends
    (Unless my sins abuse my divination)
    Success to the Roman host.

Luc.   Dream often so,
    And never false. Soft, ho ! what trunk is here ?
    Without his top ? The ruin speaks that sometime
    It was a worthy building. How ? a page ?
    Or dead, or sleeping on him ? But dead rather ;
    For nature doth abhor to make his bed
    With the defunct, or sleep upon the dead.
    Let 's see the boy's face.

Cap.   He 's alive, my lord.   360

Luc. He 'll then instruct us of this body. Young one,
    Inform us of thy fortunes, for it seems
    They crave to be demanded. Who is this
    Thou mak'st thy bloody pillow ? Or who was he
    That, otherwise than noble nature did,

Hath alter'd that good picture ? What's thy interest
In this sad wreck ? How came it ? Who is it ?
What art thou ?

Imo. I am nothing : or if not,
Nothing to be were better. This was my master,
A very valiant Briton and a good,   370
That here by mountaineers lies slain. Alas !
There is no more such masters : I may wander
From east to occident, cry out for service,
Try many, all good, serve truly, never
Find such another master.

Luc. 'Lack, good youth !
Thou mov'st no less with thy complaining than
Thy master in bleeding : say his name, good friend.

Imo. Richard du Champ. (*aside*) If I do lie, and do
No harm by it, though the gods hear, I hope
They 'll pardon it. Say you, sir ?   380

Luc. Thy name ?

Imo. Fidele, sir.

Luc. Thou dost approve thyself the very same :
Thy name well fits thy faith ; thy faith thy name :
Wilt take thy chance with me ? I will not say
Thou shalt be so well master'd, but be sure,
No less belov'd. The Roman emperor's letters
Sent by a consul to me should not sooner

Than thine own worth prefer thee : go with me.

Imo. I 'll follow, sir.   But first, an 't please the gods,   390
I 'll hide my master from the flies, as deep
As these poor pickaxes can dig : and when
With wild wood-leaves and weeds I ha' strew'd his
    grave,
And on it said a century of prayers
(Such as I can) twice o'er, I 'll weep, and sigh,
And leaving so his service, follow you,
So please you entertain me.

Luc.   Ay, good youth,
And rather father thee than master thee.
My friends,
The boy hath taught us manly duties : let us   400
Find out the prettiest daisied plot we can,
And make him with our pikes and partisans
A grave : come, arm him.   Boy, he is preferr'd
By thee to us, and he shall be interr'd
As soldiers can.   Be cheerful ; wipe thine eyes :
Some falls are means the happier to arise.   *Exeunt*

SCENE III

A room in Cymbeline's palace

Enter Cymbeline, Lords, Pisanio, and Attendants

Cym. Again ; and bring me word how 'tis with her.

Exit an Attendant

    A fever with the absence of her son ;
A madness, of which her life's in danger.   Heavens,
How deeply you at once do touch me !   Imogen,
The great part of my comfort, gone ; my queen
Upon a desperate bed, and in a time
When fearful wars point at me ; her son gone,
So needful for this present : it strikes me, past
The hope of comfort.   But for thee, fellow,
Who needs must know of her departure, and   10
Dost seem so ignorant, we'll enforce it from thee
By a sharp torture.

Pis.   Sir, my life is yours,
I humbly set it at your will : but, for my mistress,
I nothing know where she remains, why gone,
Nor when she purposes return.   Beseech your highness,
Hold me your loyal servant.

1.L.   Good my liege,
The day that she was missing, he was here ;

        I dare be bound he's true, and shall perform
        All parts of his subjection loyally.   For Cloten,
        There wants no diligence in seeking him,   20
        And will, no doubt, be found.

Cym.   The time is troublesome.
        (*to Pis.*) We'll slip you for a season, but our jealousy
        Does yet depend.

1.*L.*   So please your majesty,
        The Roman legions, all from Gallia drawn,
        Are landed on your coast, with a supply
        Of Roman gentlemen, by the senate sent.

*Cym.*Now for the counsel of my son and queen !
        I am amaz'd with matter.

1.*L.*   Good my liege,
        Your preparation can affront no less
        Than what you hear of : come more, for more you're
            ready :   30
        The want is but to put those powers in motion
        That long to move.

Cym.   I thank you : let's withdraw
        And meet the time, as it seeks us.   We fear not
        What can from Italy annoy us, but
        We grieve at chances here.   Away !

                                        Exeunt all but Pisanio

Pis. I heard no letter from my master, since

                            118

I wrote him Imogen was slain : 'tis strange :
Nor hear I from my mistress, who did promise
To yield me often tidings ; neither know I
What is betid to Cloten, but remain   40
Perplex'd in all.   The heavens still must work :
Wherein I am false, I am honest ; not true, to be true.
These present wars shall find I love my country,
Even to the note o' the king, or I 'll fall in them :
All other doubts, by time let them be clear'd :
Fortune brings in some boats that are not steer'd.

Exit

SCENE IV

Wales.   Before the cave of Belarius

Enter Belarius, Guiderius, and Arviragus

Gui. The noise is round about us.
Bel.   Let us from it.
Arv. What pleasure, sir, find we in life, to lock it
    From action and adventure ?
Gui.   Nay, what hope
    Have we in hiding us ?   This way, the Romans
    Must or for Britons slay us or receive us
    For barbarous and unnatural revolts

119

During their use, and slay us after.

Bel.   Sons,
We'll higher to the mountains, there secure us.
To the king's party there's no going: newness
Of Cloten's death (we being not known, not muster'd   10
Among the bands) may drive us to a render
Where we have liv'd, and so extort from's that
Which we have done, whose answer would be death
Drawn on with torture.

Gui.   This is, sir, a doubt
In such a time nothing becoming you,
Nor satisfying us.

Arv.   It is not likely
That when they hear the Roman horses neigh,
Behold their quarter'd fires, have both their eyes
And ears so cloy'd importantly as now,
That they will waste their time upon our note,   20
To know from whence we are.

Bel.   O, I am known
Of many in the army: many years
(Though Cloten then but young) you see, not wore him
From my remembrance.   And besides, the king
Hath not deserv'd my service, nor your loves,
Who find in my exile the want of breeding,
The certainty of this hard life, aye hopeless

To have the courtesy your cradle promis'd,
But to be still hot summer's tanlings, and
The shrinking slaves of winter.

Gui.   Than be so   30
Better to cease to be.   Pray, sir, to the army:
I and my brother are not known ; yourself
So out of thought, and thereto so o'ergrown,
Cannot be question'd.

Arv.   By this sun that shines,
I 'll thither : what thing is it that I never
Did see man die, scarce ever look'd on blood,
But that of coward hares, hot goats, and venison ?
Never bestrid a horse, save one that had
A rider like myself, who ne'er wore rowel
Nor iron on his heel ?   I am asham'd   40
To look upon the holy sun, to have
The benefit of his blest beams, remaining
So long a poor unknown.

Gui.   By heavens, I 'll go :
If you will bless me, sir, and give me leave,
I 'll take the better care ; but if you will not,
The hazard therefore due fall on me by
The hands of Romans !

Arv.   So say I : amen.

Bel. No reason I (since of your lives you set

So slight a valuation) should reserve
My crack'd one to more care. Have with you, boys!   50
If in your country wars you chance to die,
That is my bed too, lads, and there I'll lie:
Lead, lead. (*aside*) The time seems long, their blood
    thinks scorn,
Till it fly out and show them princes born. *Exeunt*

Act Fifth

SCENE I

Britain. The Roman camp

Enter Posthumus, with a bloody handkerchief

Post. Yea, bloody cloth, I'll keep thee; for I wish'd
    Thou shouldst be colour'd thus. You married ones,
    If each of you should take this course, how many
    Must murder wives much better than themselves
    For wrying but a little? O Pisanio!
    Every good servant does not all commands:
    No bond, but to do just ones. Gods, if you
    Should have ta'en vengeance on my faults, I never
    Had liv'd to put on this: so had you sav'd

The noble Imogen to repent, and struck   10
Me (wretch) more worth your vengeance.   But, alack,
You snatch some hence for little faults ; that's love,
To have them fall no more : you some permit
To second ills with ills, each elder worse,
And make them dread it, to the doers' thrift.
But Imogen is your own : do your best wills,
And make me blest to obey !   I am brought hither
Among the Italian gentry, and to fight
Against my lady's kingdom : 'tis enough
That, Britain, I have kill'd thy mistress ; peace !   20
I'll give no wound to thee.   Therefore, good heavens,
Hear patiently my purpose : I'll disrobe me
Of these Italian weeds, and suit myself
As does a Briton peasant : so I'll fight
Against the part I come with ; so I'll die
For thee, O Imogen, even for whom my life
Is, every breath, a death : and thus, unknown,
Pitied nor hated, to the face of peril
Myself I'll dedicate.   Let me make men know
More valour in me than my habits show.   30
Gods, put the strength o' the Leonati in me !
To shame the guise o' the world, I will begin
The fashion, less without and more within.   *Exit* †

SCENE II

Field of battle between the British and Roman camps

*Enter, from one side, Lucius, Iachimo, and the Roman army;
from the other side, the British army; Leonatus Posthumus following, like a poor soldier. They march over
and go out. Then enter again, in skirmish, Iachimo and
Posthumus: he vanquisheth and disarmeth Iachimo, and
then leaves him.*

Iac. The heaviness and guilt within my bosom
Takes off my manhood: I have belied a lady,
The princess of this country, and the air on't
Revengingly enfeebles me, or could this carl,
A very drudge of nature's, have subdued me
In my profession? Knighthoods and honours, borne
As I wear mine, are titles but of scorn.
If that thy gentry, Britain, go before
This lout as he exceeds our lords, the odds
Is that we scarce are men and you are gods.   *Exit* 10

*The battle continues, the Britons fly, Cymbeline is taken; then
enter, to his rescue, Belarius, Guiderius, and Arviragus*

Bel. Stand, stand, we have the advantage of the ground,
The lane is guarded: nothing routs us but
The villany of our fears.

124

Gui. ⎱   Stand, stand, and fight !
Arv. ⎰

Re-enter Posthumus, and seconds the Britons : they rescue
    Cymbeline and exeunt.   Then enter Lucius, Iachimo, and
    Imogen

Luc. Away, boy, from the troops, and save thyself ;
    For friends kill friends, and the disorder 's such
    As war were hoodwink'd.

Iac.   'Tis their fresh supplies.

Luc. It is a day turn'd strangely : or betimes
    Let 's re-inforce, or fly.   *Exeunt*

SCENE III

Another part of the field

Enter Posthumus and a British Lord

Lord. Cam'st thou from where they made the stand ?

Post.   I did :
    Though you, it seems, come from the fliers.

Lord.   I did.

Post. No blame be to you, sir, for all was lost,
    But that the heavens fought : the king himself
    Of his wings destitute, the army broken,
    And but the backs of Britons seen ; all flying

Through a strait lane, the enemy full-hearted,
Lolling the tongue with slaughtering ; having work
More plentiful than tools to do 't ; struck down
Some mortally, some slightly touch'd, some falling   10
Merely through fear, that the strait pass was damm'd
With dead men, hurt behind, and cowards living
To die with lengthen'd shame.

Lord.   Where was this lane ?

*Post.*Close by the battle, ditch'd, and wall'd with turf,
Which gave advantage to an ancient soldier
(An honest one, I warrant) who deserv'd
So long a breeding as his white beard came to,
In doing this for 's country.   Athwart the lane,
He, with two striplings (lads more like to run
The country base than to commit such slaughter,   20
With faces fit for masks, or rather fairer
Than those for preservation cas'd, or shame)
Made good the passage, cried to those that fled,
' Our Britain's harts die flying, not our men :
To darkness fleet souls that fly backwards.   Stand,
Or we are Romans, and will give you that
Like beasts which you shun beastly, and may save
But to look back in frown : stand, stand ! '   These
     three,
Three thousand confident, in act as many,—

For three performers are the file when all   30
The rest do nothing,—with this word ' Stand,
    stand,'
Accommodated by the place, more charming
With their own nobleness, which could have turn'd
A distaff to a lance, gilded pale looks,
Part shame, part spirit renew'd, that some, turn'd
    coward
But by example (O, a sin in war,
Damn'd in the first beginners !) 'gan to look
The way that they did, and to grin like lions
Upon the pikes o' the hunters.   Then began
A stop i' the chaser ; a retire ; anon   40
A rout, confusion thick : forthwith they fly
Chickens, the way which they stoop'd eagles ; slaves,
The strides they victors made : and now our
    cowards,
Like fragments in hard voyages, became
The life o' the need : having found the back-door
    open
Of the unguarded hearts, heavens, how they wound !
Some slain before, some dying, some their friends
O'er-borne i' the former wave, ten chas'd by one
Are now each one the slaughter-man of twenty :
Those that would die or ere resist are grown   50

    The mortal bugs o' the field.

Lord.   This was strange chance :
    A narrow lane, an old man, and two boys.

*Post.*Nay, do not wonder at it : you are made   †
    Rather to wonder at the things you hear
    Than to work any.   Will you rhyme upon 't,
    And vent it for a mockery ?   Here is one :
    ' Two boys, an old man twice a boy, a lane,
    Preserved the Britons, was the Romans' bane.'

*Lord.*Nay, be not angry, sir.

Post.   'Lack, to what end ?
    Who dares not stand his foe, I 'll be his friend ;   60
    For if he 'll do as he is made to do,
    I know he 'll quickly fly my friendship too.
    You have put me into rhyme.

Lord.   Farewell ; you 're angry.   *Exit*

*Post.*Still going ?   This is a lord ! O noble misery !
    To be i' the field, and ask ' what news ? ' of me !
    To-day how many would have given their honours
    To have sav'd their carcasses ! took heel to do 't,
    And yet died too ! I, in mine own woe charm'd,
    Could not find death where I did hear him groan,
    Nor feel him where he struck. Being an ugly monster, 70
    'Tis strange he hides him in fresh cups, soft beds,
    Sweet words ; or hath moe ministers than we

That draw his knives i' the war.   Well, I will find him:
For being now a favourer to the Briton,
No more a Briton, I have resum'd again
The part I came in : fight I will no more,
But yield me to the veriest hind that shall
Once touch my shoulder.   Great the slaughter is
Here made by the Roman ; great the answer be
Britons must take.   For me, my ransom 's death,   80
On either side I come to spend my breath ;
Which neither here I 'll keep, nor bear again,
But end it by some means for Imogen.

Enter two British Captains and Soldiers

1.*C.* Great Jupiter be prais'd, Lucius is taken :
   'Tis thought the old man, and his sons, were angels.

2.*C.* There was a fourth man, in a silly habit,
   That gave the affront with them.

1.*C.*   So 'tis reported
   But none of 'em can be found.   Stand ! who 's there ?

Post. A Roman,
   Who had not now been drooping here if seconds   90
   Had answer'd him.

2.*C.*   Lay hands on him ; a dog,
   A leg of Rome shall not return to tell
   What crows have peck'd them here.   He brags his
      service

As if he were of note : bring him to the king.

*Enter Cymbeline, Belarius, Guiderius, Arviragus, Pisanio,
and Roman Captives. The Captains present Posthumus
to Cymbeline, who delivers him over to a Gaoler : then
exeunt omnes*

SCENE IV

A British prison

Enter Posthumus and two Gaolers

1.*G.* You shall not now be stol'n, you have locks upon
      you :
    So graze as you find pasture.

2.*G.*   Ay, or a stomach.

                                Exeunt Gaolers

Post. Most welcome, bondage ! for thou art a way,
    I think, to liberty : yet am I better
    Than one that's sick o' the gout, since he had rather
    Groan so in perpetuity than be cur'd
    By the sure physician, death ; who is the key
    To unbar these locks. My conscience, thou art
      fetter'd
    More than my shanks and wrists : you good gods,
      give me
    The penitent instrument to pick that bolt,   10

Then free for ever !   Is 't enough I am sorry ?
So children temporal fathers do appease ;
Gods are more full of mercy.   Must I repent ?
I cannot do it better than in gyves,
Desir'd more than constrain'd : to satisfy,   †
If of my freedom 'tis the main part, take
No stricter render of me than my all.
I know you are more clement than vile men,
Who of their broken debtors take a third,
A sixth, a tenth, letting them thrive again   20
On their abatement ; that 's not my desire.
For Imogen's dear life, take mine, and though
'Tis not so dear, yet 'tis a life ; you coin'd it :
'Tween man and man they weigh not every stamp ;
Though light, take pieces for the figure's sake :
You rather mine, being yours : and so, great powers,
If you will take this audit, take this life,
And cancel these cold bonds.   O Imogen !
I 'll speak to thee in silence.   *Sleeps*

*Solemn music.   Enter, as in an apparition, Sicilius Leonatus,
    father to Posthumus, an old man, attired like a warrior,
    leading in his hand an ancient matron (his wife and
    mother to Posthumus) with music before them : then, after
    other music, follow the two young Leonati (brothers to*

*Posthumus) with wounds as they died in the wars. They
circle Posthumus round as he lies sleeping*

Sic.   No more, thou thunder-master, show   30
              Thy spite on mortal flies :
         With Mars fall out, with Juno chide,
              That thy adulteries
                   Rates and revenges.
         Hath my poor boy done aught but well,
              Whose face I never saw ?
         I died whilst in the womb he stay'd
              Attending nature's law :
         Whose father then (as men report
              Thou orphans' father art)   40
         Thou shouldst have been, and shielded him
              From this earth-vexing smart.   †

Moth.   Lucina lent not me her aid,
              But took me in my throes ;
         That from me was Posthumus ript,
              Came crying 'mongst his foes,
                   A thing of pity !

Sic.   Great nature, like his ancestry,
              Moulded the stuff so fair,
         That he deserv'd the praise o' the world,   50
              As great Sicilius' heir.

1.B.   When once he was mature for man,
            In Britain where was he
        That could stand up his parallel,
            Or fruitful object be
        In eye of Imogen, that best
            Could deem his dignity ?

Moth.   With marriage wherefore was he mock'd
            To be exil'd, and thrown
        From Leonati seat, and cast   60
            From her his dearest one,
                Sweet Imogen ?

Sic.   Why did you suffer Iachimo,
            Slight thing of Italy,
        To taint his nobler heart and brain
            With needless jealousy ;
        And to become the geck and scorn
            O' the other's villany ?

2.B.   For this, from stiller seats we came,
            Our parents and us twain,   70
        That striking in our country's cause
            Fell bravely, and were slain,
        Our fealty, and Tenantius' right,
            With honour to maintain.

133

1.*B.*   Like hardiment Posthumus hath
     To Cymbeline perform'd :
Then, Jupiter, thou king of gods,
     Why hast thou thus adjourn'd
The graces for his merits due,
     Being all to dolours turn'd ?   80

Sic.   Thy crystal window ope ; look out ;
     No longer exercise
Upon a valiant race thy harsh
     And potent injuries.

Moth.   Since, Jupiter, our son is good,
     Take off his miseries.

Sic.   Peep through thy marble mansion ; help ;
     Or we poor ghosts will cry
To the shining synod of the rest
     Against thy deity.   90

Both Bro.   Help, Jupiter ; or we appeal,
     And from thy justice fly.

*Jupiter descends in thunder and lightning, sitting upon an eagle :
    he throws a thunderbolt.   The Ghosts fall on their knees*

Jup. No more, you petty spirits of region low,
    Offend our hearing ; hush !   How dare you ghosts

Accuse the thunderer, whose bolt, you know,
　　Sky-planted, batters all rebelling coasts?
Poor shadows of Elysium, hence, and rest
　　Upon your never-withering banks of flowers:
Be not with mortal accidents opprest;
　　No care of yours it is, you know 'tis ours.　　100
Whom best I love I cross; to make my gift,
　　The more delay'd, delighted.　Be content;
Your low-laid son our godhead will uplift:
　　His comforts thrive, his trials well are spent.
Our Jovial star reign'd at his birth, and in
　　Our temple was he married.　Rise, and fade.
He shall be lord of lady Imogen,
　　And happier much by his affliction made.
This tablet lay upon his breast, wherein
　　Our pleasure his full fortune doth confine:　　110
And so away: no farther with your din
　　Express impatience, lest you stir up mine.
　　Mount, eagle, to my palace crystalline.　　*Ascends*

Sic. He came in thunder, his celestial breath
　　Was sulphurous to smell: the holy eagle
　　Stoop'd, as to foot us: his ascension is
　　More sweet than our blest fields: his royal bird
　　Prunes the immortal wing and cloys his beak,

As when his god is pleas'd.

All.   Thanks, Jupiter!

Sic. The marble pavement closes, he is enter'd   120
     His radiant roof.   Away! and, to be blest,
     Let us with care perform his great behest.

                       The Ghosts vanish

Post. (*waking*) Sleep, thou hast been a grandsire, and begot
     A father to me; and thou hast created
     A mother and two brothers: but (O scorn)
     Gone! they went hence so soon as they were born:
     And so I am awake.   Poor wretches, that depend
     On greatness' favour, dream as I have done,
     Wake, and find nothing.   But, alas, I swerve:
     Many dream not to find, neither deserve,   130
     And yet are steep'd in favours; so am I,
     That have this golden chance, and know not why.
     What fairies haunt this ground?   A book?   O rare
        one!
     Be not, as is our fangled world, a garment
     Nobler than that it covers: let thy effects
     So follow, to be most unlike our courtiers,
     As good as promise.

     (*reads*) 'Whenas a lion's whelp shall, to himself
     unknown, without seeking find, and be embrac'd by

a piece of tender air ; and when from a stately cedar 14c
shall be lopp'd branches, which, being dead many
years, shall after revive, be jointed to the old stock,
and freshly grow ; then shall Posthumus end his
miseries, Britain be fortunate and flourish in peace
and plenty.'

'Tis still a dream ; or else such stuff as madmen
Tongue, and brain not : either both, or nothing :
Or senseless speaking, or a speaking such
As sense cannot untie.   But what it is,
The action of my life is like it, which   150
I 'll keep, if but for sympathy.

Re-enter Gaolers

1.*G.* Come, sir, are you ready for death ?

Post. Over-roasted rather ; ready long ago.

1.*G.* Hanging is the word, sir, if you be ready for that,
you are well cook'd.

Post. So if I prove a good repast to the spectators, the
dish pays the shot.

1.*G.* A heavy reckoning for you, sir.   But the comfort is,
you shall be called to no more payments, fear no
more tavern-bills, which are often the sadness of 160
parting, as the procuring of mirth : you come in faint
for want of meat, depart reeling with too much

137

drink; sorry that you have paid too much, and
sorry that you are paid too much; purse and brain,
both empty; the brain the heavier for being too
light; the purse too light, being drawn of heaviness:
O, of this contradiction you shall now be quit. O,
the charity of a penny cord! it sums up thousands
in a trice: you have no true debitor and creditor
but it; of what's past, is, and to come, the dis- 170
charge: your neck, sir, is pen, book, and counters;
so the acquittance follows.

Post. I am merrier to die than thou art to live.

1.G. Indeed, sir, he that sleeps feels not the toothache:
but a man that were to sleep your sleep, and a hang-
man to help him to bed, I think he would change
places with his officer; for, look you, sir, you know
not which way you shall go.

Post. Yes, indeed do I, fellow.

1.G. Your death has eyes in 's head then; I have not seen 180
him so pictur'd: you must either be directed by some
that take upon them to know, or to take upon yourself that which I am sure you do not know, or
jump the after-inquiry on your own peril: and how
you shall speed in your journey's end, I think you 'll
never return to tell one.

Post. I tell thee, fellow, there are none want eyes to direct

them the way I am going, but such as wink, and will
not use them.

1.*G.* What an infinite mock is this, that a man should have   190
the best use of eyes to see the way of blindness !   I
am sure hanging 's the way of winking.

Enter a Messenger

Mes. Knock off his manacles, bring your prisoner to the
king.

Post. Thou bring'st good news, I am call'd to be made
free.

1.*G.* I 'll be hang'd then.

Post. Thou shalt be then freer than a gaoler ; no bolts for
the dead.   *Exeunt all but First Gaoler*

1.*G.* Unless a man would marry a gallows and beget   200
young gibbets, I never saw one so prone.   Yet, on
my conscience, there are verier knaves desire to live,
for all he be a Roman : and there be some of them
too, that die against their wills ; so should I, if I
were one.   I would we were all of one mind, and
one mind good ; O, there were desolation of gaolers
and gallowses !   I speak against my present profit,
but my wish hath a preferment in 't.   *Exit*

SCENE V

Cymbeline's tent

Enter Cymbeline, Belarius, Guiderius, Arviragus, Pisanio,
Lords, Officers, and Attendants

Cym. Stand by my side, you whom the gods have made
 Preservers of my throne. Woe is my heart,
 That the poor soldier, that so richly fought,
 Whose rags sham'd gilded arms, whose naked breast
 Stepp'd before targes of proof, cannot be found :
 He shall be happy that can find him, if
 Our grace can make him so.
Bel.   I never saw
 Such noble fury in so poor a thing ;
 Such precious deeds, in one that promis'd nought
 But beggary and poor looks.
Cym.   No tidings of him ?   10
Pis. He hath been search'd among the dead and living ;
 But no trace of him.
Cym.   To my grief, I am
 The heir of his reward, (*to Belarius, Guiderius, and*
   Arviragus) which I will add
 To you, the liver, heart, and brain of Britain,
 By whom I grant she lives. 'Tis now the time

140

To ask of whence you are : report it.

Bel.   Sir,
In Cambria are we born, and gentlemen :
Further to boast were neither true nor modest,
Unless I add, we are honest.

Cym.   Bow your knees.
Arise my knights o' the battle, I create you   20
Companions to our person, and will fit you
With dignities becoming your estates.

                    Enter Cornelius and Ladies
There's business in these faces.   Why so sadly
Greet you our victory ? you look like Romans,
And not o' the court of Britain.

Cor.   Hail, great king !
To sour your happiness, I must report
The queen is dead.

Cym.   Who worse than a physician
Would this report become ?   But I consider,
By medicine life may be prolong'd, yet death
Will seize the doctor too.   How ended she ?   30

Cor. With horror, madly dying, like her life,
Which, being cruel to the world, concluded
Most cruel to herself.   What she confess'd
I will report, so please you : these her women
Can trip me, if I err, who with wet cheeks

Were present when she finish'd.

Cym.   Prithee, say.

Cor. First, she confess'd she never lov'd you, only
Affected greatness got by you ; not you :
Married your royalty, was wife to your place ;
Abhorr'd your person.

Cym.   She alone knew this ;   40
And, but she spoke in dying, I would not
Believe her lips in opening it.   Proceed.

Cor. Your daughter, whom she bore in hand to love
With such integrity, she did confess
Was as a scorpion to her sight, whose life,
But that her flight prevented it, she had
Ta'en off by poison.

Cym.   O most delicate fiend !
Who is 't can read a woman ?   Is there more ?

Cor. More, sir, and worse.   She did confess she had
For you a mortal mineral, which, being took,   50
Should by the minute feed on life, and lingering
By inches waste you : in which time she purpos'd,
By watching, weeping, tendance, kissing, to
O'ercome you with her show ; and in time,
(When she had fitted you with her craft) to work
Her son into the adoption of the crown :
But, failing of her end by his strange absence,

Grew shameless-desperate, open'd, in despite
Of heaven and men, her purposes ; repented
The evils she hatch'd were not effected ; so   60
Despairing died.

Cym.   Heard you all this, her women ?

Ladies. We did, so please your highness.

Cym.   Mine eyes
Were not in fault, for she was beautiful,
Mine ears that heard her flattery, nor my heart
That thought her like her seeming ; it had been vicious
To have mistrusted her : yet, O my daughter
That it was folly in me, thou mayst say,
And prove it in thy feeling.   Heaven mend all !

Enter Lucius, Iachimo, the Soothsayer, and other Roman
Prisoners, guarded ; Posthumus behind, and Imogen

Thou comest not, Caius, now for tribute ; that
The Britons have raz'd out, though with the loss   70
Of many a bold one ; whose kinsman have made suit
That their good souls may be appeas'd with slaughter
Of you their captives, which ourself have granted :
So think of your estate.

Luc. Consider, sir, the chance of war, the day
Was yours by accident ; had it gone with us,
We should not, when the blood was cool, have
        threaten'd

143

Our prisoners with the sword. But since the gods
Will have it thus, that nothing but our lives
May be call'd ransom, let it come : sufficeth   80
A Roman with a Roman's heart can suffer :
Augustus lives to think on 't : and so much
For my peculiar care. This one thing only
I will entreat ; my boy (a Briton born)
Let him be ransom'd : never master had
A page so kind, so duteous, diligent,
So tender over his occasions, true,
So feat, so nurse-like : let his virtue join
With my request, which I 'll make bold your highness
Cannot deny ; he hath done no Briton harm,   90
Though he have serv'd a Roman : save him, sir,
And spare no blood beside.

Cym.   I have surely seen him :
His favour is familiar to me.   Boy,
Thou hast look'd thyself into my grace,
And art mine own.   I know not why, wherefore,
To say, live, boy : ne'er thank thy master ; live :
And ask of Cymbeline what boon thou wilt,
Fitting my bounty and thy state, I 'll give it ;
Yea, though thou do demand a prisoner,
The noblest ta'en.

Imo.   I humbly thank your highness.   100

144

Luc. I do not bid thee beg my life, good lad,
　　And yet I know thou wilt.
Imo. 　　　　　　No, no, alack,
　　There's other work in hand.　I see a thing
　　Bitter to me as death : your life, good master,
　　Must shuffle for itself.
Luc. 　　　　　　The boy disdains me,
　　He leaves me, scorns me : briefly die their joys
　　That place them on the truth of girls and boys.
　　Why stands he so perplex'd ?
Cym. 　　　　　　What wouldst thou, boy ?
　　I love thee more and more : think more and more
　　What's best to ask.　Know'st him thou look'st on ?
　　　　speak,　　　　　　　　　　　　　　　　　110
　　Wilt have him live ?　Is he thy kin ? thy friend ?
Imo. He is a Roman, no more kin to me
　　Than I to your highness, who, being born your vassal,
　　Am something nearer.
Cym. 　　　　　　Wherefore eyest him so ?
Imo. I 'll tell you, sir, in private, if you please
　　To give me hearing.
Cym. 　　　　　　Ay, with all my heart,
　　And lend my best attention.　What's thy name ?
Imo. Fidele, sir.
Cym. 　　　Thou 'rt my good youth, my page ;

I 'll be thy master : walk with me ; speak freely.

Cymbeline and Imogen converse apart

Bel. Is not this boy reviv'd from death ?

Arv.   One sand another †

Not more resembles that sweet rosy lad   121

Who died, and was Fidele.   What think you ?

Gui. The same dead thing alive.

Bel. Peace, peace ! see further ; he eyes us not ; forbear ;

Creatures may be alike : were 't he, I am sure

He would have spoke to us.

Gui.   But we saw him dead.

Bel. Be silent ; let 's see further.

Pis.   (*aside*) It is my mistress :

Since she is living, let the time run on

To good or bad.   *Cymbeline and Imogen come forward*

Cym.   Come, stand thou by our side ;

Make thy demand aloud.   (*to Iachimo*) Sir, step you
        forth,   130

Give answer to this boy, and do it freely,

Or, by our greatness and the grace of it,

Which is our honour, bitter torture shall

Winnow the truth from falsehood.   On, speak to him.

Imo. My boon is that this gentleman may render

Of whom he had **this** ring.

Post.   (*aside*) What 's that to him ?

Cym. That diamond upon your finger, say
    How came it yours?

Iac. Thou 'lt torture me to leave unspoken that
    Which, to be spoke, would torture thee.

Cym.   How! me? 140

Iac. I am glad to be constrain'd to utter that
    Which torments me to conceal.   By villany
    I got this ring : 'twas Leonatus' jewel ;
    Whom thou didst banish ; and (which more may
        grieve thee,
    As it doth me) a nobler sir ne'er liv'd
    'Twixt sky and ground.   Wilt thou hear more, my
        lord?

Cym. All that belongs to this.

Iac.   That paragon, thy daughter,
    For whom my heart drops blood, and my false spirits
    Quail to remember—Give me leave ; I faint.

Cym. My daughter? what of her? Renew thy strength.   150
    I had rather thou shouldst live while nature will
    Than die ere I hear more : strive, man, and speak.

Iac. Upon a time—unhappy was the clock
    That struck the hour !—it was in Rome,—accurst
    The mansion where !—'twas at a feast,—O, would
    Our viands had been poison'd, or at least
    Those which I heav'd to head !—the good Posthumus,—

What should I say ? he was too good to be
Where ill men were, and was the best of all
Amongst the rar'st of good ones—sitting sadly,   160
Hearing us praise our loves of Italy
For beauty, that made barren the swell'd boast
Of him that best could speak ; for feature, laming
The shrine of Venus, or straight-pight Minerva,
Postures beyond brief nature ; for condition,
A shop of all the qualities that man
Loves woman for, besides that hook of wiving,
Fairness which strikes the eye—

Cym.   I stand on fire :
Come to the matter.

Iac.   All too soon I shall,
Unless thou wouldst grieve quickly.   This Posthumus,
Most like a noble lord, in love, and one   171
That had a royal lover, took his hint,
And (not dispraising whom we prais'd, therein
He was as calm as virtue) he began
His mistress' picture, which, by his tongue being made,
And then a mind put in 't, either our brags
Were crack'd of kitchen-trulls, or his description
Prov'd us unspeaking sots.

Cym.   Nay, nay, to the purpose.

Iac. Your daughter's chastity—there it begins.

He spake of her, as Dian had hot dreams,   180
And she alone were cold : whereat I, wretch,
Made scruple of his praise, and wager'd with him
Pieces of gold 'gainst this, which then he wore
Upon his honour'd finger, to attain
In suit the place of 's bed, and win this ring
By hers and mine adultery : he, true knight,
No lesser of her honour confident
Than I did truly find her, stakes this ring,
And would so, had it been a carbuncle
Of Phœbus' wheel ; and might so safely, had it   190
Been all the worth of 's car.   Away to Britain
Post I in this design : well may you, sir,
Remember me at court, where I was taught
Of your chaste daughter the wide difference
'Twixt amorous and villanous.   Being thus quench'd
Of hope, not longing, mine Italian brain
'Gan in your duller Britain operate
Most vilely ; for my vantage, excellent ;
And, to be brief, my practice so prevail'd,
That I return'd with simular proof enough   200
To make the noble Leonatus mad,
By wounding his belief in her renown
With tokens thus, and thus ; averring notes
Of chamber-hanging, pictures, this her bracelet,—

O cunning, how I got it !—nay, some marks
Of secret on her person, that he could not
But think her bond of chastity quite crack'd,
I having ta'en the forfeit.   Whereupon—
Methinks I see him now—

Post.   (*advancing*) Ay, so thou dost,   210
Italian fiend !   Ay me, most credulous fool,
Egregious murderer, thief, any thing
That 's due to all the villains past, in being,
To come !   O, give me cord, or knife, or poison,
Some upright justicer !   Thou, king, send out
For torturers ingenious ; it is I
That all the abhorred things o' the earth amend
By being worse than they.   I am Posthumus,
That kill'd thy daughter : villain-like, I lie,
That caus'd a lesser villain than myself,
A sacrilegious thief, to do 't.   The temple   220
Of virtue was she ; yea, and she herself.
Spit, and throw stones, cast mire upon me, set
The dogs o' the street to bay me : every villain
Be call'd Posthumus Leonatus, and
Be villany less than 'twas !   O Imogen !
My queen, my life, my wife !   O Imogen,
Imogen, Imogen !

Imo.   Peace, my lord ; hear, hear—

*Post.*Shall 's have a play of this ?   Thou scornful page,
    There lie thy part.   *Striking her : she falls*

Pis.   O, gentlemen, help !
    Mine and your mistress !   O, my lord Posthumus !   230
    You ne'er kill'd Imogen till now.   Help, help !
    Mine honour'd lady !

Cym.   Does the world go round ?

*Post.*How comes these staggers on me ?

Pis.   Wake, my mistress !

*Cym.*If this be so, the gods do mean to strike me
    To death with mortal joy.

Pis.   How fares my mistress ?

Imo. O, get thee from my sight ;
    Thou gavest me poison : dangerous fellow, hence !
    Breathe not where princes are.

Cym.   The tune of Imogen !

Pis. Lady,
    The gods throw stones of sulphur on me, if   240
    That box I gave you was not thought by me
    A precious thing : I had it from the queen.

*Cym.*New matter still ?

Imo.   It poison'd me.

Cor.   O gods !
    I left out one thing which the queen confess'd,
    Which must approve thee honest : ' If Pisanio

Have,' said she, ' given his mistress that confection
Which I gave him for cordial, she is serv'd
As I would serve a rat.'

Cym.   What 's this, Cornelius ?

Cor. The queen, sir, very oft importun'd me
To temper poisons for her, still pretending   250
The satisfaction of her knowledge only
In killing creatures vile, as cats and dogs,
Of no esteem : I, dreading that her purpose
Was of more danger, did compound for her
A certain stuff, which being ta'en would cease
The present power of life, but in short time
All offices of nature should again
Do their due functions.   Have you ta'en of it ?

Imo. Most like I did, for I was dead.

Bel.   My boys,
There was our error.

Gui.   This is sure Fidele.   260

Imo. Why did you throw your wedded lady from you ?
Think that you are upon a rock, and now   †
Throw me again.   *Embracing him*

Post.   Hang there like fruit, my soul,
Till the tree die !

Cym.   How now, my flesh, my child ?
What, makest thou me a dullard in this act ?

Wilt thou not speak to me?

Imo.   (*kneeling*) Your blessing, sir.

Bel. (*to Gui. and Arv.*) Though you did love this youth,
        I blame ye not;
You had a motive for 't.

Cym.   My tears that fall
    Prove holy water on thee!   Imogen,
    Thy mother's dead.

Imo.   I am sorry for 't, my lord.   270

Cym. O, she was naught; and long of her it was
    That we meet here so strangely: but her son
    Is gone, we know not how nor where.

Pis.   My lord,
    Now fear is from me, I 'll speak troth.   Lord Cloten,
    Upon my lady's missing, came to me
    With his sword drawn, foam'd at the mouth, and swore,
    If I discover'd not which way she was gone,
    It was my instant death.   By accident,
    I had a feigned letter of my master's
    Then in my pocket, which directed him   280
    To seek her on the mountains near to Milford,
    Where, in a frenzy, in my master's garments
    (Which he enforc'd from me) away he posts
    With unchaste purpose, and with oath to violate
    My lady's honour: what became of him

    I further know not.

Gui.   Let me end the story:
I slew him there.

Cym.   Marry, the gods forfend!
I would not thy good deeds should from my lips
Pluck a hard sentence: prithee, valiant youth,
Deny 't again.

Gui.   I have spoke it, and I did it.   290

Cym. He was a prince.

Gui. A most incivil one: the wrongs he did me
Were nothing prince-like; for he did provoke me
With language that would make me spurn the sea,
If it could so roar to me: I cut off 's head;
And am right glad he is not standing here
To tell this tale of mine.

Cym.   I am sorry for thee:
By thine own tongue thou art condemn'd, and must
Endure our law: thou 'rt dead.

Imo.   That headless man
I thought had been my lord.

Cym.   Bind the offender,   300
And take him from our presence.

Bel.   Stay, sir king:
This man is better than the man he slew,
As well descended as thyself, and hath

More of thee merited than a band of Clotens
Had ever scar for.   *(to the Guard)* Let his arms alone,
They were not born for bondage.

Cym.   Why, old soldier,
Wilt thou undo the worth thou art unpaid for,
By tasting of our wrath ?   How of descent
As good as we ?

Arv.   In that he spake too far.

Cym. And thou shalt die for 't.

Bel.   We will die all three :   310
But I will prove that two on 's are as good
As I have given out him.   My sons, I must
For mine own part unfold a dangerous speech,
Though haply well for you.

Arv.   Your danger 's ours.

Gui. And our good his.

Bel.   Have at it then, by leave.
Thou hadst, great king, a subject who
Was call'd Belarius.

Cym.   What of him ? he is
A banish'd traitor.

Bel.   He it is that hath
Assum'd this age ; indeed a banish'd man,
I know not how a traitor.

Cym.   Take him hence,   320

155

The whole world shall not save him.

Bel.   Not **too hot**:
First pay me for the nursing of thy sons,
And let it be confiscate all, so soon
As I have receiv'd it.

Cym.   Nursing of my sons?

Bel. I am too blunt and saucy: here's my knee:
Ere I arise, I will prefer my sons,
Then spare not the old father.   Mighty sir,
These two young gentlemen that call me father,
And think they are my sons, are none of mine,
They are the issue of your loins, my liege,   330
And blood of your begetting.

Cym.   How? my issue?

Bel. So sure as you your father's.   I (old Morgan)
Am that Belarius whom you sometime banish'd:
Your pleasure was my mere offence, my punishment †
Itself, and all my treason: that I suffer'd
Was all the harm I did.   These gentle princes
(For such and so they are) these twenty years
Have I train'd up: those arts they have as I
Could put into them; my breeding was, sir, as
Your highness knows.   Their nurse, Euriphile   340
(Whom for the theft I wedded) stole these children
Upon my banishment: I mov'd her to 't,

156

Having receiv'd the punishment before
For that which I did then : beaten for loyalty
Excited me to treason : their dear loss,
The more of you 'twas felt, the more it shap'd
Unto my end of stealing them.   But, gracious sir,
Here are your sons again, and I must lose
Two of the sweet'st companions in the world.
The benediction of these covering heavens   350
Fall on their heads like dew, for they are worthy
To inlay heaven with stars.

Cym.   Thou weep'st, and speak'st.
The service that you three have done is more
Unlike than this thou tell'st.   I lost my children :
If these be they, I know not how to wish
A pair of worthier sons.

Bel.   Be pleas'd awhile.
This gentleman, whom I call Polydore,
Most worthy prince, as yours, is true Guiderius :
This gentleman, my Cadwal, Arviragus,
Your younger princely son ; he, sir, was lapp'd   360
In a most curious mantle, wrought by the hand
Of his queen mother, which for more probation
I can with ease produce.

Cym.   Guiderius had
Upon his neck a mole, a sanguine star,

157

It was a mark of wonder.   †

Bel.   This is he,
Who hath upon him still that natural stamp:
It was wise nature's end in the donation,
To be his evidence now.

Cym.   O, what am I?
A mother to the birth of three? Ne'er mother
Rejoic'd deliverance more. Blest pray you be,   370
That, after this strange starting from your orbs,
You may reign in them now! O Imogen,
Thou hast lost by this a kingdom.

Imo.   No, my lord;
I have got two worlds by 't. O my gentle brothers,
Have we thus met? O, never say hereafter
But I am truest speaker: you call'd me brother,
When I was but your sister; I you brothers,
When ye were so indeed.

Cym.   Did you e'er meet?
Arv. Ay, my good lord.
Gui.   And at first meeting lov'd,
Continued so, until we thought he died.   380
Cor. By the queen's dram she swallow'd.
Cym.   O rare instinct!
When shall I hear all through? This fierce abridgement
Hath to it circumstantial branches, which

Distinction should be rich in.   Where ? how liv'd
    you ?
And when came you to serve our Roman captive ?
How parted with your brothers ? how first met
    them ?
Why fled you from the court ? and whither ?   These,
And your three motives to the battle, with
I know not how much more, should be demanded,
And all the other by-dependances,   390
From chance to chance : but nor the time nor place
Will serve our long inter'gatories.   See,
Posthumus anchors upon Imogen ;
And she, like harmless lightning, throws her eye
On him, her brothers, me, her master, hitting
Each object with a joy : the counterchange
Is severally in all.   Let 's quit this ground,
And smoke the temple with our sacrifices.
(*to Belarius*) Thou art my brother, so we 'll hold thee
    ever.

Imo. You are my father too, and did relieve me,   400
To see this gracious season.

Cym.   All o'erjoy'd,
Save these in bonds ; let them be joyful too,
For they shall taste our comfort.

Imo.   My good master,

I will yet do you service.

Luc.   Happy be you !

Cym. The forlorn soldier, that so nobly fought,
He would have well become this place, and grac'd
The thankings of a king.

Post.   I am, sir,
The soldier that did company these three
In poor beseeming ; 'twas a fitment for
The purpose I then follow'd.   That I was he,   410
Speak, Iachimo : I had you down, and might
Have made you finish.

Iac.   (*kneeling*) I am down again :
But now my heavy conscience sinks my knee,
As then your force did.   Take that life, beseech you,
Which I so often owe : but your ring first,
And here the bracelet of the truest princess
That ever swore her faith.

Post.   Kneel not to me :
The power that I have on you is to spare you ;
The malice towards you, to forgive you : live,
And deal with others better.

Cym.   Nobly doom'd !   420
We 'll learn our freeness of a son-in-law ;
Pardon 's the word to all.

Arv.   You holp us, sir,

As you did mean indeed to be our brother ;
Joy'd are we that you are.

Post. Your servant, princes.   Good my lord of Rome,
Call forth your soothsayer : as I slept, methought
Great Jupiter, upon his eagle back'd,
Appear'd to me, with other spritely shows
Of mine own kindred : when I wak'd, I found
This label on my bosom ; whose containing   430
Is so from sense in hardness, that I can
Make no collection of it : let him show
His skill in the construction.

Luc.   Philarmonus !

Sooth. Here, my good lord.

Luc.   Read, and declare the meaning

Sooth. (*reads*) 'Whenas a lion's whelp shall, to himself
unknown, without seeking find, and be embrac'd by
a piece of tender air ; and when from a stately
cedar shall be lopp'd branches, which, being dead
many years, shall after revive, be jointed to the old
stock, and freshly grow, then shall Posthumus end   440
his miseries, Britain be fortunate and flourish in
peace and plenty.'
Thou, Leonatus, art the lion's whelp ;
The fit and apt construction of thy name,
Being Leo-natus, doth import so much.

(*to Cymbeline*) The piece of tender air, thy virtuous
    daughter,
Which we call ' mollis aer ' ; and ' mollis aer '
We term it ' mulier ' : which ' mulier ' I divine
Is this most constant wife, who even now,
Answering the letter of the oracle,   450
Unknown to you, unsought, were clipp'd about
With this most tender air.

Cym.   This hath some seeming.
Sooth. The lofty cedar, royal Cymbeline,
Personates thee : and thy lopp'd branches point
Thy two sons forth ; who, by Belarius stol'n,
For many years thought dead, are now reviv'd,
To the most majestic cedar join'd, whose issue
Promises Britain peace and plenty.

Cym.   Well ;
My peace we will begin. And, Caius Lucius,
Although the victor, we submit to Cæsar,   460
And to the Roman empire ; promising
To pay our wonted tribute, from the which
We were dissuaded by our wicked queen ;
Whom heavens in justice both on her and hers
Have laid most heavy hand.
Sooth. The fingers of the powers above do tune
The harmony of this peace. The vision,

Which I made known to Lucius ere the stroke
Of this yet scarce-cold battle, at this instant
Is full accomplish'd ; for the Roman eagle,   470
From south to west on wing soaring aloft,
Lessen'd herself, and in the beams o' the sun
So vanish'd : which foreshow'd our princely eagle,
The imperial Cæsar, should again unite
His favour with the radiant Cymbeline,
Which shines here in the west.

Cym.   Laud we the gods,
And let our crooked smokes climb to their nostrils
From our blest altars.   Publish we this peace
To all our subjects.   Set we forward : let
A Roman and a British ensign wave   480
Friendly together : so through Lud's town march,
And in the temple of great Jupiter
Our peace we 'll ratify ; seal it with feasts.
Set on there !   Never was a war did cease,
Ere bloody hands were wash'd, with such a peace.

                                                    Exeunt

Notes

I. i. 1-3. *our bloods . . .*; the trap in this slightly obscure sentence is the word *more*; in modern idiom the phrase would mean that the bloods do not obey the heavens at all; here it means that the imitation-flattery of the courtiers is no less exact than the obedience of tempers to planetary influences, *i.e.* that it is complete.

I. i. 31. *Tenantius*; Cymbeline's father.

I. i. 49. *feated*; no satisfactory emendation; the sense is clear, that he was a model (as in *Hamlet, the glass of fashion*).

I. i. 116. *sear*; the F *seare* is no doubt a variant spelling of 'cere,' *i.e.* to wrap in 'cere-cloths'; but the conjecture *seal* is tempting.

I. ii. 18. *Puppies !*; I feel that this ought to be singular; the lord has no intention of sneering at Posthumus, as the plural makes him.

I. iv. 57. *qualified*; this word presents a real difficulty; the obvious hyphenation, adopted by many, *constant-qualified*, though Shakespearean enough as a word, seems to me to ruin the rhythm of the sentence; but to take *qualified* as meaning no more than 'equipped with good qualities' seems a feebly general anti-climax.

I. vi. 36. *number'd*; if this is right it must mean just 'numerous.' But Theobald's *th' unnumber'd* is tempting (cf. *Lear*, IV. vi. 21, *the unnumber'd idle pebbles*).

I. vi. 104. *Fixing*; this is the usual emendation for F's *Fiering*, from which it is hard to extract a reasonable meaning.

I. vi. 109. *unlustrous*; Rowe's reading for F's *illustrious*; the latter can be clumsily justified with the sense 'just so far illustrious as . . . ,' *i.e.* not illustrious at all.

165

I. vi. 121. *to be partner'd . . .*; *i.e.* to think that a lady like you should have as your equals in his affection the prostitutes that your own money enables him to pay.

II. ii. 18. *do't*; if this is right it must mean ' kiss.'

II. ii. 45. *tale of Tereus*; Tereus, king of Thrace, married to Progne, violated her sister, Philomela, and cut out her tongue. She worked her story on a sampler and sent it to her sister, who then killed her son Itylus and cooked him as a dish for her husband.

II. iii. 25. *pretty is*; I have not ventured to alter the reading, but there is much to be said for Hanmer's *pretty bin*. He is de-cried for wanting to produce an unnecessary rhyme; but after the strong chime on *sings* and *springs* in the first four lines one's ear is certainly expecting a recurrence of the rhyme-scheme in the second.

II. iii. 48. *soliciting*; F reads *solicity*, for which the reading of the text is the more usual emendation; but I suspect that F2's *solicits* (noun) is the better conjecture.

II. iv. 24. *mingled*; so F 2. F reads *wing-led*, and though the hyphen is suspicious, and, as Craig points out, *wingled* is in Q 1 of *Richard III* applied to Mercury, who can hardly be *mingled*, nevertheless the sense of *mingled* is so much nearer to what is wanted that I accept it. I have ventured to read *courage* for F's *courages*. The singular is needed not only for easy scansion, but (more important) for the run of the sentence, after *courage* two lines above; and this text shows several examples of an intrusive final *s*, e.g. ll. 138 and 140 of the preceding scene, where F reads *His garments* the first time and the clearly right *garment* the second.

II. iv. 83. *the cutter . . .*; this means, I suppose, that the carver was equal to nature, but dumb (*i.e.* could not give speech), and indeed surpassed her in the actual figures, if one left out of the reckoning that he could not endow the figures with speech and motion. But the run of the sentence is slightly awkward, it does not easily carry on from *so likely to report themselves*, and I suspect something lurking beneath *another*.

· II. v. 16. *a German one*; F reads *a Iarmen on*. The emendation is Rowe's, but it cannot be thought satisfactory, unless one could find some more significant sense of 'German' as applied to a boar than has hitherto been advanced. In view of the crude brutality of Posthumus' expressions I feel that Singer is on the right lines in wanting to read *briming* ('brime' being 'a term among hunters, when the wild boar goeth to the female') though the actual reading is impossible to justify graphically.

II. v. 27. *may be nam'd*; so F 2 for F's *name*. Graphically the best emendation is Vaughan's *name may name*, but it is hardly so good in sense.

III. i. 19. *As Neptune's park . . .*; F reads *ribb'd and pal'd in With Oakes . . .* The double *ed* ending is, I think unnatural, and it may be that something has dropped out altogether; e.g. *ribb'd and pal'd in, for oaks, With rocks . . .*

III. iii. 6. *turbans*; Johnson pointed out that the readers of romances always confounded the idea of a giant with that of a Saracen.

III. iii. 23. *bauble*; so Rowe, usually accepted for F's *Babe*. Hanmer read *bribe*. Rowe's reading is graphically much the easier, since *bauble* was frequently spelt *bable*.

III. iv. 3. *as I have now. Pisanio! man!*; various attempts have been made to explain this as it stands. But, apart from the awkwardness of the metre, the sense is oddly incomplete, and I think that it is a reasonable conjecture that a whole line has dropped out. I do not think that *I have* need be suspect; the shift from 'long'd' to 'have longing' is not un-Shakespearean. But something like

> *To see me first, as I have now to see*
> *My wedded lord; how now, Pisanio, man !*

would give the expected sense, and the dropping of the line, the compositor's eye being caught both by *so* (? *soe*) and *see* and the repeated *now*, would be easy. (I do not advance this as a 'conjecture'; but it perhaps illustrates how readers, when they feel a passage unsatisfactory, can play the game for themselves according to some sort of rules of probability.)

III. iv. 51. *whose mother was her painting*; there have been many emendations. If we stick to the text the only possible meaning seems to be 'who gets her looks from her painting, not from her mother'; but this is admittedly not satisfactory; nor are the emendations.

III. iv. 59, 60. *Aeneas* was false to Dido, queen of Carthage; *Sinon* was the Greek who by his false tale of misery convinced the Trojans of his truth, and persuaded them to bring the wooden horse into the city.

III. iv. 80. *afore't*; Rowe's emendation of F's pointless *a-foot*.

III. iv. 103. *wake my eye-balls blind first*; so Hanmer. F reads simply *wake my eye-balls first*, which is neither metre nor sense. The text gives no doubt the required sense, though a word nearer in appearance to *first* or to *balls* would be graphically easier than *blind*.

III. iv. 134. *that harsh, noble, simple nothing,*; so F, except that it reads a colon for the comma after *nothing*. Something is clearly wrong here, and there have been many conjectures. *Noble* is suspicious, since Imogen, apart from the fact that she could hardly call Cloten 'noble' (as adjective) except in awkward irony, would not naturally call the Queen's son a 'noble.' Otherwise we might try *harsh noble, noble simply in nothing.* I think that the trouble is beyond the cure of legitimate conjecture.

III. vi. 69. *but be your groom*; *i.e.* 'rather than miss being.' The punctuation is F's. Many editors put a colon or the like after *groom*, and no stop, or a comma, after *honesty.* Dowden makes the excellent suggestion that *I* before *bid* should be omitted: the insertion would be easy from the line above. Alternatively we might read *Ay, bid . . .*

III. vi. 76. *prize*; if this is right the phrase means 'the prize of me.' But we should probably read either *price* (Hanmer) or *peize* (Vaughan). In any case I do not think that Imogen means 'if I had been a rustic girl, my prize would have been less' (Dowden), *i.e.* 'if I had been the daughter of their father,' which seems an unnecessary, though not at all impossible, wrench of the sense, but just what she says, *i.e.* 'if they had been my father's sons (who are lost) I should not be his only heir.'

IV. i. 14. *imperseverant*; so F, and no one knows what it means. Dyce's *imperceiverant* (*i.e.* 'obtuse') is described as a happy correction, but its happiness is a trifle clouded when we find that the word is otherwise unknown. But 'perceiverance' occurs, and in the spelling 'perseverant'; so that Dyce was probably right.

IV. ii. 206. *crare*; the brilliant, though not perhaps certain, conjecture of Sympson for F's *care*; a *crare* is a small trading-vessel.

IV. ii. 207. *easilest*; so F (and for that matter F 2), so suggesting that the word presented no difficulties. I retain it, not only on general principles, but because it seems to suggest some light on the vexed passage in *The Tempest*, III. i. 15.

V. i. 33. *The fashion . . .*; *i.e.* 'the new fashion of "less show and more substance."'

V. iii. 53. *Nay, do not wonder* . . .; a curious passage; if it is right as it stands, Posthumus must apparently mean 'don't wonder at it; but it is no good saying that to you, since you are a person made to wonder at report rather than do anything worth wondering at when reported.' In any case his outburst is surprising at a natural enough remark of the lord's.

V. iv. 15. *Desir'd* . . .; if we are to take the passage as it stands, some sort of meaning can be wrested from it. 'The gyves are welcome rather than forced upon me. If I am to give satisfaction, and that is the way to secure the freedom that matters (of conscience, not of body, *cf.* ll. 8, 9) take no more limited forfeit from me than all I have (*i.e* my life); (or, 'no more stringent forfeit' since there cannot be one more stringent than all I have).

V. iv. 42. *earth-vexing*; possibly we should read with Vaughan *heart-vexing*.

V. v. 120. *One sand another*. . .; so F, except that it prints a colon after *lad*. There has been a pother of needless conjecture; the ellipse 'One sand another not more resembles (than this boy resembles) that sweet rosy lad' is surely thoroughly Shakespearean. But even though the punctuation of this play is uncertain there the colon is, and I am inclined to think that Dowden was right in following (with modifications) Johnson, making it a case of 'transposed pointing,' and reading *One sand another Not more resembles : that sweet rosy lad Who died, and was Fidele.*

V. v. 262. *upon a rock*; apart from graphical difficulties (*l* and *r* not being easily confoundable) Dowden's conjecture of *lock*, *i.e* the wrestling hold, seems to have everything to commend it.

V. v. 334. *Your pleasure* . . .; this passage seems to me beyond hope. F reads *neere* for *mere*, but that is, if anything, worse. The first phrase is interpreted to mean 'my only offence was in your caprice,' but 'pleasure' is a weak word for caprice, and anyway, on Belarius' own showing (III. iii. 66), it was not a matter of caprice; Cymbeline had evidence, even if the evidence was false. For Belarius to say that what he suffered was all the harm he did is absurd, since he is just admitting that he stole the king's sons, even though he justifies it by a kind of perverted logic as an offence that followed rather than preceded its punishment. It seems to me better to admit frankly that the passage is incomprehensible than to make Shakespeare responsible for a kind of 'English unseen.'

V. v. 365. *It was a mark of wonder*; there is a small point here which is of no importance to the text, but is perhaps worth comment, as showing how easily errors creep into a text and may become perpetuated. F reads, as here, *was*; so does the (Aldis Wright) Cambridge edition. But the Temple edition, printed from that Cambridge edition, and the Arden edition, printed from a collation of the Folios by so careful a scholar as Dowden, both read (without comment) *is*, a reading so damaging to the sense that even if the Folio had read it it would have inevitably been emended.

Glossary

MANY words and phrases in Shakespeare require glossing, not because they are in themselves unfamiliar, but for the opposite reason, that Shakespeare uses in their Elizabethan and unfamiliar sense a large number of words which seem so familiar that there is no incentive to look for them in the glossary. It is hoped that a glossary arranged as below will make it easy to see at a glance what words and phrases in any particular scene require elucidation. A number of phrases are glossed by what seems to be, in their context, the modern equivalent rather than by lexicographical glosses on the words which compose them.

Act First

SCENE I

line
6 REFERR'D, given
13 TO THE BENT, to copy
22 COMPARE, challenge comparison
25 WITHIN HIMSELF, short of his deserts
33 SUR-ADDITION, sur-name
37 FOND OF, doting on
53 HER ELECTION, her choice of him

line
63 CONVEY'D, stolen away
124 SEE, *sc. each other*
126 FRAUGHT, burden
129 REMAINDERS, people who remain
135 SENSELESS OF, insensible to
140 PUTTOCK, kite
149 NEAT-HERD, cow-herd

SCENE II

11 WAS IN DEBT, (?) skulked like a debtor

23 ELECTION, choice

SCENE III

24 WITH HIS NEXT VANTAGE, the first chance he has

32 ENCOUNTER ME WITH ORISONS, be at prayers when I am

173

SCENE IV

line

2 CRESCENT NOTE, rising reputation
6 TABLED, recorded
18 UNDER HER COLOURS, on her side
19 EXTEND, extol
28 KNOWING, experience, knowledge of 'good form'
33 KNOWN TOGETHER, been acquainted

line

37 ATONE, reconcile
39 IMPORTANCE, prompting
89 CASUAL, a matter of chance
106 MOIETY, half
122 APPROBATION, proof
134 RELIGION, scruple

SCENE V

64 CORDIAL, life-giving
77 REMEMBRANCER, reminder

80 LIEGERS, 'resident ambassadors'
81 HUMOUR, mood

SCENE VI

22 NOTE, repute
37 PARTITION, distinction
   SPECTACLES, (?) powers of vision
38 ADMIRATION, wonder
98 DISCOVER, disclose
108 BY PEEPING IN, glancing sideways with
121 TO BE, to think that she should be
122 EXHIBITION, allowance

123 VENTURES, venturers
134 RAMPS, drabs
151 MART, bargain
152 STEW, brothel
177 FAN, test (winnow)
191 CURIOUS, anxious
200 SHORT, come short of
208 TENDER OF OUR PRESENT, trend of my present business

Act Second

SCENE I

2 UP-CAST, the 'wood' of the next player
23 CAPON, chicken (type of stupidity)

26 UNDERTAKE, 'take on'
27 COMPANION, fellow

174

SCENE II

line   line

38 CINQUE-SPOTTED, five-spotted

SCENE III

2 ACE, the lowest throw in dice
16 CONCEITED, well thought-out
31 UNPAV'D, without 'stones' (*i.e.* castrated)
42 MINION, darling
49 SEASON, occasion
98 KNOWING, experience
120 SELF-FIGUR'D, self-chosen
121 ENLARGEMENT, freedom

122 CONSEQUENCE, succession
123 NOTE, repute
124 FOR, suitable for
125 PANTLER, servant who looked after bread
130 COMPARATIVE FOR, corresponding with
135 CLIPP'D, embraced
140 SPRITED, haunted

SCENE IV

71 OR, either
73 BRAVELY, stylishly
87 FRETTED, carved
    ANDIRONS, 'dogs' in fireplace
88 WINKING, with eyes shut
90 NICELY, well-balanced

91 BRANDS, torches
107 BASILISK, serpent reputed to kill with glance of eye
133 COLTED, ravished
151 PERVERT, divert

SCENE V

20 MOTION, impulse

26 NICE, wanton

Act Third

SCENE I

31 GIGLET, strumpet
36 MOE, more (*Eliz. plur.*)
37 OWE, own

47 INJURIOUS, insulting
50 AGAINST ALL COLOUR, without excuse

SCENE II

line
21 FEODARY, confederate
28 CHARACTERS, handwriting
33 MEDICINABLE, medicinal (*active*)
39 TABLES, tablets

line
55 BATE, keep control of myself
57 THICK, fast
78 FRANKLIN, yeoman farmer

SCENE III

5 JET, strut
17 APPREHEND, understand
20 SHARDED, with wing-cases
26 UNCROSS'D, with the debt not struck out

35 STRIDE A LIMIT, overstep a boundary
40 BEASTLY, like beasts
57 REPORT, reputation
73 FORE-END, earlier part

SCENE IV

17 TAKE OFF SOME EXTREMITY, mitigate the sharpness of a blow
50 FAVOUR, appearance
61 SCANDAL, cast doubt on
63 LAY THE LEAVEN ON, infect

122 ABUS'D, deceived
123 SINGULAR, past-master
157 NICENESS, fastidiousness
159 IT, its
165 TITAN, the sun-god

SCENE V

35 SLIGHT, easy

164 MEED, reward

SCENE VI

23 CIVIL, civilized
28 WOODMAN, hunter
34 RESTY, restless

78 WRINGS AT, is tortured by
86 OUT-PEER, surpass

SCENE VII

15 SUPPLIANT, auxiliary

Act Fourth

SCENE I

line
21 OF, over

line

SCENE II

8 CITIZEN, city-bred
10 JOURNAL, daily
50 CHARACTERS, letters
59 SPURS, roots
61 WITH THE INCREASING VINE, (?) as the vine grows
75 KNOCK, blow
93 MERE, complete
107 ABSOLUTE, certain
110 FELL, fierce
133 HUMOUR, mood
134 MUTATION, mutability

185 CLOTPOLL, head
225 RUDDOCK, robin
230 WINTER-GROUND, cover against frost (as a plant with straw)
281 CONSUMMATION, conclusion (*i.e.* death)
294 PITTIKINS, *dim. of* pity
316 IRREGULOUS, lawless
321 MAIN-TOP, maintopmast
338 CONFINERS, inhabitants
403 PREFERR'D, recommended

SCENE III

22 SLIP, let go free

23 DEPEND, hang over you

SCENE IV

6 REVOLTS, rebels
11 RENDER, disclosure

18 QUARTER'D, of their bivouacs
33 O'ERGROWN, covered with hair

Act Fifth

SCENE I

5 WRYING, going astray

CYMBELINE

SCENE III

SCENE IV

SCENE V